RETURN OF THE SEA OTTER

RETURN OF THE
SEA OTTER

THE STORY OF THE ANIMAL THAT EVADED
EXTINCTION ON THE PACIFIC COAST

Todd McLeish

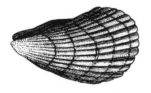

SASQUATCH BOOKS
SEATTLE

Printed in the United States of America

Published by Sasquatch Books

22 21 20 19 18   9 8 7 6 5 4 3 2 1

Editor: Gary Luke
Production editor: Bridget Sweet
Design: Bryce de Flamand
Copyeditor: Kirsten Colton
Front cover illustration: Donna McKenzie
Interior photographs: Michael Yang, Michael L. Baird, Sean Crane, Kim Steinhardt, Ken Conger, Renay McLeish, and Patrick J. Endres/AlaskaPhotoGraphics.com
Interior and back cover illustrations: © iStock.com | nicoolay – Seafood Illustrations, © iStock.com | bauhaus1000 – Seashell and Sea Life Engraving

Library of Congress Cataloging-in-Publication Data
    Names: McLeish, Todd, author.
    Title: Return of the sea otter : the story of the animal that evaded
        extinction on the Pacific Coast / Todd McLeish.
    Description: Seattle, WA : Sasquatch Books, [2018] | Includes bibliographical
        references and index.
    Identifiers: LCCN 2017041436 | ISBN 9781632171375 (paperback : alk. paper)
    Subjects: LCSH: Sea otter--Conservation--Pacific Coast (North America)
    Classification: LCC QL737.C25 M36 2018 | DDC 333.95/976950979--dc23
    LC record available at https://lccn.loc.gov/2017041436

ISBN: 978-1-63217-137-5

Sasquatch Books
1904 Third Avenue, Suite 710
Seattle, WA 98101 | (206) 467-4300
www.sasquatchbooks.com

SUSTAINABLE FORESTRY INITIATIVE

Certified Sourcing
www.sfiprogram.org
SFI-01268

SFI label applies to text stock only

For Renay, yet again

Contents

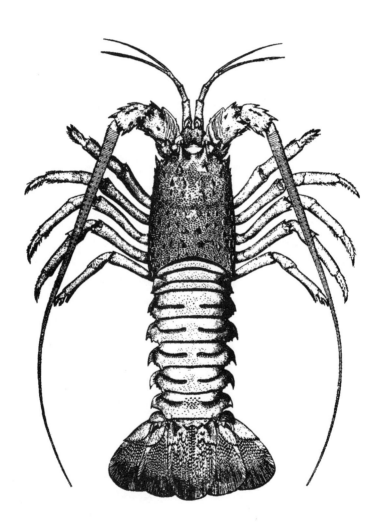

Introduction

~~~~~~~~~~~

KARL MAYER is adamant that sea otters are not cute—not the tiny fluff balls in their first days and weeks of life, not the chocolate-covered juveniles, not the grizzled adults. We should take his opinion seriously, as he has been rescuing and rehabilitating sea otter pups and adults for more than twenty years at the Monterey Bay Aquarium, including spending many years as a wet suit–attired surrogate mother teaching them to find food in the wild. So he should know what he's talking about. As a result of his work, Mayer has been bitten and scarred numerous times by the sometimes vicious sea otters, which is probably the main factor in his unpopular opinion.

But he is wrong. Judging by the oohs and aahs and coos and sighs I hear at the very mention of the words "sea otter," the animals are the definition of cute. In fact, cute may be an understatement. Even the fishermen whose livelihoods are jeopardized by the recolonization of sea otters admit that their nemesis rates at the top of the cuteness scale, and probably always will. Dozens of online videos of sea otters holding hands, pups resting on their floating mothers, otters wrapped in kelp, and otters pounding open shellfish with rocks on their bellies—viewed by tens of millions of adoring fans—will ensure their reputation for cuteness in perpetuity.

In my three years of studying sea otters, interviewing scientists, and observing otters in the wild in preparation for writing this book, I made a conscious effort to avoid the *C* word so as to maintain my credibility with the experts and remain as unbiased as possible about the conflicts otters cause and the wrath they sometimes incur. But I failed miserably. I accidentally let slip the words "cute" and "adorable" too many times to count in aquarium settings, at research facilities, and while tracking the animals in the wild. I couldn't help myself. Despite Mayer's assertion, otters are cuter than the proverbial button. And I'm happy to admit it. I don't know whether it's their furry bodies and whiskered faces, their humanlike grooming skills, their use of their belly as a picnic table, or their delightful childcare strategies that have earned them the moniker "the champions of cute"—it's more likely a combination of all of those traits, but I'm not about to disagree with the sentiment of the majority.

The cuteness of sea otters and the ease with which they can be viewed in central California, southern Alaska, and dozens of aquariums worldwide make them immensely popular among a broad audience. The market for sea otter T-shirts, mugs, charms, and trinkets, not to mention sea otter–based ecotourism, is huge, and they are one of the primary drivers of the economy in and around Monterey, California. It doesn't hurt that more than two dozen children's books have been published about sea otters in the last twenty years, creating multiple generations of sea otter fans far beyond their limited range along the North Pacific coastline.

Their cuteness aside, however, sea otters are remarkable creatures who exert a dramatic positive influence on the health of at least two very different marine ecosystems, and their unique physiology and tool use make them stand out among the world's marine mammals. Yet the otter has also faced centuries of murderous persecution for its lustrous fur coat, which became the foundation of an immensely profitable trade with China that quickly led to the animal's extirpation throughout most of its range and to its near extinction at the beginning of the twentieth century. Otters remain controversial in many places, especially in Southeast Alaska, as they recolonize more and more of their former range and deplete a variety of marine invertebrates that had built to unnaturally high populations in their absence. Commercial fisheries had become established for some of those abundant invertebrates, like sea urchins, sea cucumbers, and several species of crabs, but the sea otters' return often reduces the commercial harvest of these invertebrates to unviable levels. The otters are also unfairly blamed for invertebrate declines more appropriately attributed to overfishing and other causes. The increasing numbers of sea otters in some regions have fueled calls for lethal control—and even a bounty by one legislator in Alaska—to restore invertebrate populations to their prior unnatural levels. But over time the animals tend to win over most people, and in most places the establishment of a growing wildlife-watching industry soon far surpasses the economic value of the fisheries. Yet the animals remain disliked by a small but vocal segment of the human population that refuses to acknowledge the value in their appeal. For those individuals, the cuteness of sea otters will never trump their perceived deficiencies.

I was drawn to sea otters during numerous wildlife-watching vacations to California and Alaska in my thirties and forties. I distinctly remember my conversion from birder to sea otter aficionado during a trip in the late 1990s to Morro Bay, California, a three-hour drive north of Los Angeles. The bay's epicenter is Morro Rock, a massive geologic pinnacle my bird guides indicated was an ideal site for observing canyon wrens, white-throated swifts, and nesting peregrine falcons. While we found our target species and got especially good looks at the falcons, it was a group of about fifteen sea otters in a cove leading to the rock that was most memorable. The animals appeared unafraid of people as they lounged on their backs close to the roadway, within easy viewing and photography range. The photos my wife, Renay, and I shot that day remain among the best wildlife photos we have ever taken. And there was no doubt in either of our minds that those animals were adorable. Whenever we recall that trip, it's the otters that remain most distinct in our memories.

Since then we have sought out sea otters several more times in Monterey Bay and Seward, Alaska, experiences that convinced me to write this book. My research took me back to Seward, as well as to the Aleutian Islands, Homer, Juneau, and Prince of Wales Island in Alaska; to Vancouver and Vancouver Island in British Columbia; to the Olympic Peninsula of Washington; and up and down the central coast of California. During those travels, I helped numerous scientists with their research; observed sea otter autopsies and surgeries; met with fishermen and Native Alaskans unhappy about the growing population of sea otters; watched sea otters from a kayak, sailboat, motel room, cliff, restaurant, and research vessel; visited several aquariums where otters were being rehabilitated and exhibited; and interviewed dozens of sea otter biologists and enthusiasts. Those experiences gave me an even greater appreciation for the natural history—and the associated controversies—of the cutest animal on earth.

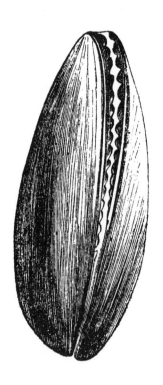

Chapter 1: Keystone Species

ALMOST IMMEDIATELY upon submerging, we came upon a forest unlike any I had ever seen, a forest of complex textures and stunning colors that quickly enveloped us and pulled us deeper into its multilayered environment. The trees were small and scattered at first, just several pencil-thick stalks of golden kelp woven into thin trunks that soared skyward. Fronds of feathery leaves reached toward the water's surface every foot or so along each stalk, sometimes dancing in the surging tides or, at the surface, floating to support the weight of hungry birds. As we entered the forest, it became increasingly dense, with uncountable stalks joining together to form massive trunks, alarmingly entangling our feet and hands and leaving little space to maneuver. The roots of this forest, called holdfasts, appeared as an explosion of sticky, skinny fingers grasping the rocky seafloor but never digging into the sediments. Scattered at the forest's edge were great meadows of fluffy purple sand dollars standing erect in the sand, like columns of soldiers aligned for battle.

I was on my first scuba dive in eight years, my first dive ever in the Pacific Ocean, and my guides for the day were introducing me to the underwater world of Monterey Bay, along the central coast of California, where numerous marine reserves help to protect a dynamic ecosystem and a spectacular array of ocean life. We were just two hundred yards from tourist shops and restaurants yet in a world far more impressive and majestic than most in the crowds could even imagine. Just as John Steinbeck described in his novel about the area, *Cannery Row*, "the sea is very clear, and the bottom becomes fantastic with hurrying, fighting, feeding, breeding animals."

Attached to the rocks supporting the kelp were patches of iridescent algae, fist-size maroon blades that flashed pink and purple in the penetrating sunlight. And between the seaweeds were tiny animals almost too breathtaking to be real. Slug-like nudibranchs of several varieties—including an out-of-range southern species decked out in magenta with yellow stripes, a more subdued lemony specimen, and the showy Hopkin's rose, whose wavy, bright-pink gills made it look like a clown's wig—were difficult to spot nestled in hiding places in the rocks. The most impressive, though, was the pale-pink-and-orange rainbow nudibranch, three times as large as the others, a showy, writhing creature that feeds on tube anemones.

Nearby we came across groups of brown sea hares, football-size slugs on steroids that congregate in groups of six or eight, often surrounding giant plates of their yellow, spaghetti-like eggs. Bat stars in autumnal colors were seemingly everywhere, and ghostly decorator crabs covered in living algae and anemones lurked mostly unseen. My guides, Scott Bernasconi and Michelle Stamme, pointed out several tiny red octopuses; camouflaged a mottled sandy color rather than their namesake red, they were barely noticeable until they moved slightly or sought refuge in dime-size clam holes. As we wandered the seafloor, dodging the giant kelp while investigating rocky crevices where fluorescent-purple sea urchins lurked beside the largest starfish I have ever seen, we spied anemones of every imaginable color, scary-looking sheep crabs and cabezon fish, and a massive gumboot chiton resembling a hard loaf of bread with a fleshy yellow underside.

About twenty-five minutes into our dive, I experienced some difficulties with my scuba gear, so I signaled to Bernasconi and Stamme to return to the surface. As we ascended to the canopy, we passed hovering rockfish and kelpfish, kelp crabs and grazing turban snails. We emerged into the bright sunshine for a brief conversation and minor equipment adjustment. Before submerging again, we took a quick glance around, and not twenty yards from us was a resting sea otter wrapped in kelp, its silky bay-colored fur highlighted by a mocha head and a hint of amber on its snout. Its mittened paws were crossed on its chest as if praying, its rear flippers were raised out of the water to absorb the warmth of the sun, and its pelage still dripped from a recent foraging dive. It was a teddy bear–like animal, cuddly and charismatic, and in defiance of our proximity, it ignored us completely—probably because it was sound asleep.

The animal didn't remain sleeping long. It must have sensed our presence, because a few moments later it opened its chocolate eyes, raised its head, and glared at us. Despite our alien-like scuba outfits, the otter seemed only mildly annoyed by our too-close-for-comfort manifestation. It was obviously used to being awoken by divers, kayakers, and other intruders. It glanced quickly around to confirm that we were the only ones encroaching on its territory, then swiveled its head back in my direction as if to reassure itself that we weren't dangerous. And still in a reclining position, as if nothing was amiss, it proceeded to groom itself.

The sea otter first tossed aside a blade of kelp, no longer needing it to remain in place, then dipped its nimble paws in the water and began rubbing its cheeks. After rinsing its paws again, it moved on to massaging its scalp, ears, and neck before moistening its digits one more time and rubbing its eyes. It then grabbed a handful of fur from its chest and tugged it toward its mouth, whereupon it spent a few seconds licking the fur into shape before repeating the process with a different patch. It followed the same procedure a few more times, tugging and licking and tugging and licking, until each hair was apparently clean and in the right position. The otter then gave its upper body a quick shake, like a dog exiting the tub, stretched its lanky body, and returned to a reclining position. With one more glance at me and my companions, it flashed a toothy grin and went back to sleep.

We watched the otter for a minute or two more as we drifted silently toward it, trying to decide whether to continue our dive or abandon it in favor of more otter watching. Although we chose to return to the seafloor, we paused to give homage to the sea otter because we knew it was the otter that was responsible for nearly everything else we were to see that day.

SEA OTTERS (*Enhydra lutris*) have an unusual influence on the health and maintenance of their kelp-forest ecosystem. In their absence, the kelp forest declines rapidly as a result of what scientists refer to as a trophic cascade—a domino effect in which the demise of one species affects the health or behavior of another species until almost all have been disturbed. We often hear about how species are linked in a food web and how each has an ecological role to play, but in most cases the ecosystem can sustain itself after the loss of a few species. But that's not true of sea otters and kelp forests. When sea otters are removed from a kelp forest, the population of one of the otters' favorite foods, sea urchins, expands rapidly, and the urchins, which prefer the taste of kelp, quickly consume the luxuriant seaweed, mowing down everything sprouting from the rocky seafloor. With no kelp, the kelpfish and kelp crabs and just about every other species I saw on my dive—and many more—disappear entirely, leaving a barren landscape like an abandoned nuclear test site. But return sea otters to the ecosystem, and a revolution ensues as the otters keep the urchins in check, allowing the kelp to make a comeback. This is followed by the crabs and snails and nudibranchs and schools of fish that then attract sea lions, rounding out the resurrection of the kelp forest. This cascade of species rises and falls entirely because the sea otter plays such a crucial role in the function of its ecosystem.

While that makes sea otters ecologically important, they are much more than that. Sea otters are all about superlatives. They are the smallest of the world's marine mammals, yet considerably larger than one would imagine from their photographs, with males growing to a length of five feet or more. Sometimes topping out at more than one hundred pounds, they are the heaviest members of the Mustelidae family, which includes skunks, weasels, badgers, and wolverines. They have the densest fur of any animal on earth, with as many as one million hairs per square inch of fur, compared to the one hundred thousand hairs that typical humans have on their entire head. The sea otter is the only marine mammal with no blubber, the only Mustelid that does not dig a den or burrow, the only marine mammal that uses its paws rather than its mouth to capture prey, and the only marine mammal capable of lifting and overturning rocks to find food. And it is one of very few mammals known to use tools. It's no wonder why otters are so adored.

But they are so much more than just the sum of their super-latives, too. One of thirteen otter species around the world, sea otters are believed to have evolved from primitive, fish-eating otter ancestors in Eurasia about five to seven million years ago. Those ancestors were probably terrestrial mammals that moved into the marine environment relatively recently—whale, dolphin, and seal ancestors took to the sea between fifteen and forty million years earlier—perhaps to escape from predators or to gain access to more abundant prey resources, like the invertebrates they likely discov-ered while foraging at low tide. That's probably when they began to evolve the specific adaptations that allow them to spend most of their lives in the ocean, including rear flippers to aid in underwater locomotion, the ability to survive without consuming freshwater, an expanded lung capacity enabling them to dive beneath the sur-face for food, and strategies for giving birth and raising their young entirely at sea.

Fossil evidence suggests that the sea otter genus became con-fined to the North Pacific one to three million years ago, with records from the early Pleistocene collected from Cape Blanco, Oregon, and Moonstone Beach, California. The only surviving member of the genus, today's modern sea otter, is believed to have evolved along the coast of eastern Russia and northern Japan before spreading across the arc of Alaska's Aleutian Islands and down the coast of North America.

Living primarily in kelp-forest habitat in nearshore waters—though they sometimes use soft-sediment areas and other habi-tats as well—sea otters are seldom found more than a mile from shore. Estimates of their pre–fur trade numbers range from 150,000 to 300,000, but just a few remnant populations totaling fewer than 1,000 animals survived into the twentieth century.

Naturally recovering populations and reintroductions into former habitat resulted in a 2015 world population of about 125,000 sea otters living in scattered locations including the coasts of central California, Washington, British Columbia, Southeast Alaska, Prince William Sound, the Aleutian Islands, and Russia's Commander Islands.

They aren't all exactly alike, though. Three subspecies are recognized: the southern sea otter, found exclusively in central California; the northern sea otter, ranging from Washington to Alaska; and the common or Asian sea otter, found on the Commander Islands, the Kuril Islands of the western Pacific, and occasionally the northernmost islands of Japan. Although the Asian subspecies has long been considered the largest otter and the southern subspecies the smallest, there are actually few physical differences among them. In fact, their physical size has more to do with the availability of food than genetic differences. Sea otters living in areas where food is abundant in California are likely to be larger than otters found in areas of Alaska where food is limited, for instance, even though California otters are, on average, slightly smaller than Alaska otters.

When food is available, sea otters are voracious eaters. They have to be. Because they have no blubber to keep them warm in the chilly waters of the North Pacific, they must consume 25 to 30 percent of their body weight in food every day. Were I in the same boat, I would have to eat nearly forty pounds of food each day just to maintain my weight. To accomplish this feat, sea otters feed on a wide range of benthic marine invertebrates, including sea urchins, clams and other mollusks, crabs of many varieties, sea cucumbers, abalone and other snails, and occasionally even fish and seabirds. As a result of their prodigious appetite, they often control prey populations and can make commercial harvest of some species unviable. That renders them especially unpopular among some fishermen, who find it impossible to compete with the highly adapted and unrestricted sea otter for several economically valuable species. But far from being entirely negative, the ability of sea otters to keep some marine invertebrates—especially sea urchins—from growing too abundant has provided benefits to entire ecosystems and made them the quintessential representative of what scientists call keystone species.

Sea otters are apex predators in their kelp-forest habitat. They are at the top of the food chain and exert an extraordinary influence on the composition of other species found there. That influence is something discovered in the 1970s by Jim Estes, the dean of sea otter researchers in North America for the last half century. He says that keystone species are those that are "relatively rare but very important ecologically." He compared two islands in the Aleutian chain in Alaska—Amchitka, where sea otters were abundant, and Shemya, where sea otters were hunted to extinction more than a century before—and he found dramatic differences that he concluded were the result of the sea otters' influence. For the next several decades, he watched those and other North Pacific sites with and without otters and made an extensive variety of comparisons. Everywhere he went he found the same thing: where sea otters were plentiful, the kelp-forest ecosystem was healthy and home to numerous other species; where otters were absent, the ecosystem became what he called an "urchin barren" with hardly any kelp left at all and few other thriving species. He discovered that barnacles and mussels grew three or four times faster in kelp forests than in urchin barrens, and some species of fish could be ten times more abundant where otters and kelp were present. And it was not just the underwater world that was affected. Glaucous-winged gulls flying at the surface changed their diet in the absence of otters and kelp, switching from about 90 percent fish to 90 percent inverte-brates. Bald eagles made a similar adjustment in their diet from fish, marine mammals, and seabirds when otters were present to mostly seabirds when they were not. Estes even found that sea otters influenced the carbon cycle, the movement of carbon as it is used and recycled in biogeochemical processes from the atmo-sphere to the oceans and back.

"We've come to the view that the whole base of the structure and function of the ecosystem is influenced by the impact of otters through this trophic cascade," Estes told me. "That, in retrospect, is a fairly predictable and not surprising finding, because when you take the plants out of the system, which is essentially what happens when you lose otters"—urchins eat all the kelp—"you're going to influence almost everything about that system. Just like if you were to go in and clear-cut a forest, you would be hard pressed to find a species that wasn't influenced by that. That's pretty much the kind of process we're talking about here."

Beyond their role as a keystone species in the kelp forests of the coastal North Pacific, sea otters exhibit a number of other unique characteristics that make them much more similar to unrelated marine mammals than to their closer terrestrial cousins. Rather than having flesh-tearing teeth more typical of other carnivores, they have adaptations to their teeth and jaws enabling them to bite with tremendous force and crush their hard-shelled prey. They are capable of diving more than three hundred feet beneath the sea sur-face, thanks to the increased oxygen-storage capacity of their large lungs and an anaerobic metabolism, similar to that in whales and seals, when especially long or deep dives are necessary. And their loosely articulated skeleton and absent clavicle enable them to be unusually flexible, providing them access via their paws and mouth to every inch of skin for whole-body grooming and for whatever movements may be necessary in their aquatic environment. Their reproductive traits have also evolved to be more similar to that of marine mammals than their relatives on land, including giving birth to a single young (rarely to twins), gestating for a relatively long period of six months, and caring for young for an extended time. Living up to twenty-five years in captivity but more often ten to fifteen years in the wild, socially they are more like marine mammals as well, gathering in sometimes large groups—usually sexually segregated—to rest and, less often, to feed.

Perhaps, however, sea otters are most celebrated for their tool use, a skill that places them, among mammals, in the company of only humans, chimpanzees, and dolphins. Who wouldn't be charmed by a furry creature that carries a tool—a rock, most often, but driftwood, glass bottles, and other objects as well—in a purselike pouch in its armpit while it forages for hard-shelled prey, then uses the tool to crack open that prey while reclining on its back in the water? And when an appropriate-size tool isn't available, they're known to get creative by smacking shellfish against marina docks, jetties, boat hulls, and any other hard surface they can access. One study of abalone shell breakage patterns in California in the late 1960s found 80 percent of the shells had been broken by a tool likely used by a sea otter. Yet tools are used by the otters not only once they have brought their prey to the surface, but to dislodge prey from underwater rocks or crevices. Otters have also been known to begin the process of cracking open shelled prey while still submerged.

Like jazz musicians, sea otters must constantly improvise how they use particular tools, developing new and inventive ways to gain access to their prey. The most common method is to use their belly like a picnic table, placing a rock there and smashing the prey down on the tool. They sometimes also reverse the process and use the rock as a hammer against the prey. And they have even been observed using one rock like an anvil on their belly, placing the prey item upon it, and then using a second rock to crack open the shell. When part of a shell is finally broken off, that piece often becomes a tool to further pound on the already-broken prey. And sometimes sea otters may slam one shelled animal against another until both of them reveal their flesh. As scientists spend more and more time observing sea otter foraging behavior, they are discovering an even wider variety of strategies for tool use. I'm especially intrigued by the otters that use different strategies for different prey, like one animal that used a rock for cracking turban snails and a glass bottle for prying mollusks off an underwater ledge.

Beyond the impressive tool use, though, beyond the cuteness factor, beyond even the sea otter's dramatic influence on its habitat, if you're still not enamored of the sea otter, then perhaps its incredible fur coat will make you a fan. The animal's thick pelt has led to massive human changes: sea otter fur was indirectly responsible for the establishment of a global mercantile industry, the alteration of Native American cultures, the accusation that Russians enslaved Native hunters, the first use of firearms by Natives on the British Columbia coast, the first Russian settlements on the Aleutian Islands, the deaths of hundreds (perhaps thousands) of seamen from a half dozen countries, and the establishment of new trade routes, not to mention the animal's near extinction. All because of its fur.

But what amazing fur it is. Thanks to their pelt, sea otters don't need blubber to keep them warm in the icy North Pacific (though their rapid metabolism helps them stay warm, too). A freshly groomed otter has the same insulating capacity as a harbor seal with a thick layer of blubber. In fact, according to Heather Liwanag, a biology professor at Adelphi University who has compared the insulating qualities of fur and blubber, sea otters would need a layer of blubber larger than themselves to equal the insulating abilities of their pelt. Maintaining that pelt is quite a job, though. Sea otters must spend hours each day grooming themselves and blowing air into their fur to increase its thermoregulation properties, because it's the layer of trapped air in their fur that provides the insulating power. It also makes them extremely buoyant, however, so to dive deep the animals must release some of the trapped air in a stream of bubbles as they submerge.

Amazingly, despite living their entire lives in the water, sea otters almost never get their skin wet. Each sea otter hair is covered in tiny geometric barbs that help to mat the hairs together so tightly that water cannot penetrate to the skin. A dry otter—even when it's in the water—is a warm otter. But that pelt of matted fur is a lot to carry around with them. When removed from its body, that fur coat—consisting of an inner insulating layer of very short, soft underfur protected by long outer guard hairs—represents about one quarter of the animal's weight. It's like a human wearing a forty-pound coat around just to keep the chill off, and then being unable to remove it when the temperature rises. Lucky for the otters, their watery habitat never gets too warm.

UNFORTUNATELY, that luxurious fur has historically been the sea otter's greatest vulnerability, and in some places it remains so today. Demand for sea otter furs among merchants in Canton, China, in the late 1700s and early 1800s drove the animals to near extinction as a result of an active ship-based trading system that developed throughout the North Pacific. For more than half a century, Russian, British, and American merchant ships competed for access to sea otter pelts harvested mostly by Native peoples from California to the outer reaches of Alaska and beyond.

Demand for furs of all varieties was high in China, and prior to the European exploration of the North Pacific and the northwest coast of North America, that demand was primarily met by Russian traders, who delivered as many as a million furs each year—primarily otter, lynx, squirrel, fox, and sable—from Siberia to China. In the 1760s, Russia began a commercial expansion eastward across the Aleutian Islands, and by the end of the decade, all of the Aleutians had been explored for their potential to yield valuable furs that could be sold in China. Sea otter pelts were found to be the most valuable fur by far. A handful of well-financed Russian merchants established permanent settlements on some islands, hired local Natives to capture sea otters, and eventually banded together to establish the Russian-American Company to control the Alaska fur trade.

By then, though, British and American merchants heard about the money that could be made from sea otter pelts in China and rushed to Alaska and British Columbia to enter what would become known as the North West Coast trade. British captain James Cook's third voyage of discovery explored the coast of Alaska and the Bering Strait, and along the way acquired sea otter pelts for one shilling apiece that, in 1779, they traded in China for $120 (or a profit of 1,800 percent). When unauthorized reports of Cook's voyage were published in Britain and New England several years later, the rush was on to trade European and American trinkets, raw materials, guns, and textiles with the North West Coast Natives for sea otter pelts, which were then traded to Chinese merchants for tea, silks, porcelain, and other products that were in great demand back in European and American ports.

Sea otter pelts were quickly considered the most desirable and most valuable furs in the world, used primarily to line winter clothing. The best were glossy black and could be more than five feet long and three feet wide. The Chinese graded sea otter pelts in up to ten classes, while the Russians subdivided them into four categories based on the size of the pelt and the length and softness of the fur. Pelts from Russia's Kuril Islands and Kamchatka Peninsula were considered the best—which led to the otters in that region becoming extirpated first—followed by otter furs from the Aleutian Islands, the North West Coast, and California.

Native groups along coastal Alaska and British Columbia, including Chinook, Nootka, Salish, Haida, and Tlingit people, prized sea otter pelts for their warmth and beauty long before the coastal trade began. Some tribes allowed only their chiefs and other leaders to wear clothing made from sea otter fur. But the animals weren't easy to hunt—it was considered more dangerous than whaling—because sea otters are smart, cagey, excellent swimmers, and aggressively defensive of their young. Yet because they were already skilled otter hunters, it was relatively easy for the Natives to intensify their hunting effort to meet the demands of the trading vessels.

Initially, the Native peoples traded furs to acquire iron for making fishhooks, arrowheads, knife blades, and lance tips, and copper for fashioning into bracelets and other adornments. Later they sought cotton cloth, firearms, molasses, and rum. In 1796, one otter skin brought two yards of blue cloth at Clayoquot Sound and six yards at Nootka Sound, both on the west coast of Vancouver Island. But by 1826, when sea otters had become scarce, the price was twelve yards of cloth. One ship visiting the Queen Charlotte Islands (now Haida Gwaii) in 1812 was reported to have traded four blankets, four buckets of molasses and rice, an axe, and other gifts for one sea otter skin.

In the early going, it was the Russians who led the trade by employing what many considered the best sea otter hunters, Native Aleuts and Kodiak Islanders. Unlike the Americans and British, who only traded and transported furs, the Russians commanded hundreds of Alaska Natives to hunt for them in kayaks. The hunters would typically be directed to start in March or April, with upwards of 150 kayaks setting out from Kodiak Island, 100 from Unalaska Island, and 50 from Atka Island (and sometimes smaller numbers from Cook Inlet and Prince William Sound), and proceed to designated locations along the coast, where they stayed through the summer. At the end of the season, they submitted the animals they harvested for three to thirty rubles per skin, depending on the grade of the pelt.

When the British entered the trade following Cook's voyage, the rush for otter skins was on. In 1785, Captain James Hanna and a crew of thirty were the first to arrive, having traveled around South America to Nootka Sound on a sixty-ton brig renamed the *Sea Otter*. They acquired 560 otter skins in five weeks and sold them in China a year later for $24,000. By then six other British ships were trading along the North West Coast, including several that were led by former members of Cook's expedition, one of whom claimed that "the fur trade is inexhaustible wherever there are inhabitants." But British involvement in the fur trade all but ended by the turn of the nineteenth century, primarily due to conflicts with the East India Company and the South Sea Company, which had monopolies on British trade in the Pacific and in China. By the time the trade monopolies were abolished in 1834, there were few otters left to buy and fur was falling out of fashion.

For much of the period, the trade was dominated by American ships, most of which originated in Boston. Throughout the 1790s, American vessels annually traded goods valued, on average, at about $62,000 to acquire from Native groups furs that brought in $350,000 in China. A decade later, the value of the furs in China was three or four times greater. But by the 1810s, the trade slowed because too many ships were chasing too few otters. And while the fur trade continued for several more decades, the financial return declined dramatically as sea otters became more and more scarce. By 1841, the last of the American vessels withdrew and the trade was all but over.

The sea otter trade in California was over even earlier. It started in 1785, soon after the discovery of San Francisco Bay, and it was initially led by the Spanish, who were primarily interested in keeping the northern coast unexplored as a buffer against foreign infiltration into Southern California and Mexico. Spain even issued regulations governing otter hunting, but the trade there didn't thrive. The California Natives were not skilled sea otter hunters and seemed uninterested in becoming so, since they had no need for furs in the warm climate. After 1800, American ships dominated the trade in California, even after the Russians arrived in 1809 and explored for otters as far south as Baja California when the animals were depleted in California waters. But by the 1820s, the California fur rush spiraled downward.

In a history written of the Russian-American Company, it was reported that Russian traders sold nearly seventy-three thousand sea otter furs to China—along with thirty-four thousand beavers, fifteen thousand river otters, and more than one hundred thousand foxes of several varieties—between 1797 and 1821. Over a similar period, American vessels made 127 voyages from the North West Coast to China, and during the peak four years, nearly sixty thousand sea otter pelts were imported to China, along with twice as many beaver furs and ten times as many fur seal skins. It wasn't until 1911 that sea otter hunting was finally banned by the International Fur Seal Treaty, but by then 123 ships had reported killing 198,284 sea otters, completely wiping out most populations. So it's no wonder that one hundred years later the hapless sea otter remains a species of great concern.

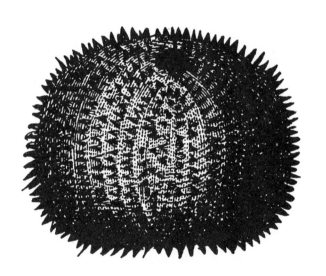

Chapter 2: Opposition

AT THE END of the fur trade, hardly a sea otter was to be found in all of California, Oregon, Washington, British Columbia, or Southeast Alaska. Thirteen small populations of otters were thought to have survived into the early 1900s in widely scattered groupings, mostly from Prince William Sound, Alaska, west across the Aleutian Islands. Some contained just a handful of animals, though, and not all of the groups survived for very long. It would take many decades filled with numerous gains and losses before sea otters returned to most of their historic range and their numbers were healthy again. In some places they still face hardships and controversies. Yet based on the conversations I have had with dozens of people, from schoolchildren to senior citizens, and the many more I have observed at aquariums and viewing sites, sea otters have achieved a level of popularity surpassed by few other animals.

But their popularity isn't universal. In fact, the range of emotions inspired by sea otters runs the gamut from joy to hatred, depending largely on whether you perceive them to have a negative economic effect. And in California, that range of emotions has been displayed often in public meetings, regulatory hearings, and protests for more than fifty years. While the overwhelming public sentiment is now largely in favor of the otters, it wasn't always that way.

Passage of the International Fur Seal Treaty of 1911 and the US Fur Seal Act of 1912 provided a level of protection to the few sea otters that survived the fur trade, although the latter legislation protected them only in waters beyond three miles offshore, where hardly any otters roamed. A year later, the state of California passed legislation to fully protect sea otters within its boundaries. By then, however, it was believed that sea otters had been completely extirpated from the state, down from about sixteen thousand before the fur trade. But it wasn't long before staff of the California Department of Fish and Game (now Department of Fish and Wildlife) discovered a group of about fifty sea otters not far south of Carmel in Big Sur, a stretch of rugged and remote coastline where the Santa Lucia Mountains rise from the Pacific Ocean. According to Lilian Carswell, the southern sea otter recovery coordinator for the US Fish and Wildlife Service, that was when those governing the state of California first became proponents of sea otters. "They loved them and wanted to protect them and thought of them as this precious little jewel that had survived beyond all odds," she said.

California Fish and Game officers were said to have carefully guarded the animals, and ranchers in the area even kept an eye out for them by reporting sightings of poachers. The otters' existence remained a well-kept secret for more than twenty years until Highway 1 opened between San Simeon and Monterey and provided the public with easy access to the coastline. In 1938, the otters were officially rediscovered by Mr. and Mrs. H. G. Sharpe when, as the story goes, they were testing a newly repaired telescope at the bridge over Bixby Creek along the Big Sur coast and observed a number of sea otters. By then the otter population was believed to be 100 to 150 animals, though later estimates have suggested there could have been as many as 300. Local residents became so concerned that the animals could be harmed that they insisted Fish and Game officials assign a warden to guard them. Three years later, the state established the California Sea Otter Game Refuge, a region encompassing the entire known range of the animals at that time and within which it was illegal to possess firearms. The otters expanded their range, and the refuge was expanded in 1959 to encompass the entire coast from the Carmel River in the north to Santa Rosa Creek in the south.

During the century or so that sea otters were almost entirely absent from their former range along the California coast, populations of marine invertebrates like abalone, Dungeness crabs, and sea urchins had increased to levels of abundance not previously recorded in nature. Without the otters around to keep them in check, these invertebrates were found in such great numbers that commercial fisheries became established. And when the otters began to return to their previous haunts in the 1940s, '50s, and '60s and shared in the harvest, the fishermen were not pleased. It was the abalone fishermen who were initially the most vocal.

Abalones are marine snails in the genus *Haliotis* that are related to oysters, clams, and other shellfish. They are primitive creatures with simple anatomies and live in large domed shells described by some as ear shaped. (*Haliotis* means "sea ear.") Eight of the 130 species worldwide are found in California, where some species grow as large as ten inches in diameter. Abalones live on the rocky seafloor in kelp forests and amid other seaweeds, ranging from the intertidal zone to as deep as five hundred feet, though most are found in shallow waters.

Chinese immigrants started the abalone industry on the California coast in the 1860s, and by 1879, they were harvesting as much as four million pounds of meat and shell per year, primarily red, green, and black abalone, the three species found closest to shore. Populations of those species quickly became depleted, prompting some California counties to establish laws prohibiting the harvesting of abalones except in deeper water. That's when Japanese immigrants became the major players in the industry by using abalone-harvesting methods from their home country—deep-diving suits and dive helmets—that allowed them to access abalone farther offshore. When Japanese Americans were forced into internment camps during World War II, Caucasian divers took over the industry, working from boats tended by crew members who followed the divers as they walked on the seafloor and collected their catch. After the fishery reached its peak of 5.4 million pounds in 1957, it slowly began to decline. The fishermen, of course, blamed the decline on the growing population of sea otters expanding their range. But that was only a small part of the story.

IN THE LATE 1940s, the abalone fishermen had begun to voice their displeasure over the competition they faced from sea otters, and by the 1960s they had gained the attention of enough local politicians that the California Senate Fact Finding Committee on Natural Resources established a subcommittee on sea otters. A public hearing in 1963 on the effect of sea otters on abalones was intended to seek input about the biology and ecology of sea otters and the perceived economic impact they were having on the abalone industry. Chaired by Senator Fred Farr of Monterey, the hearing was attended by a large assemblage representing environmental groups, abalone divers, academic biologists, staff of the California Department of Fish and Game, and many others, including Margaret Owings, a conservationist and resident of Big Sur who would later start the influential nonprofit group Friends of the Sea Otter.

In their testimony, the fishermen tried to paint a picture of the devastation they claimed the sea otters left in their wake—nothing but broken, empty abalone shells in areas that had previously been highly productive fishing areas. One fisherman said that before sea otters had arrived in the waters off the town of Gorda, he had harvested 176 dozen abalone during a one-day trip in 1947, while another claimed to have regularly taken 40 dozen abalone every few months for several years in the area of the San Simeon lighthouse until the sea otters arrived. They apparently didn't consider that the vast numbers of abalone they were harvesting could have any effect on the sustainability of the abalone population.

Environmentalists and natural-resource managers in attendance at the hearing did their best to correct some of the fishermen's claims. Several, including *National Geographic* photographer Tom Myers, provided a historical perspective that the fishermen had ignored. "The sea otter and the abalone lived together for who knows how many millions of years before us, and the sea otter never wiped out the abalone," he said. Others suggested that it was the human harvest of abalone that was the real problem and that the sea otters were simply being made a scapegoat, especially when considering that the number of licensed abalone fishermen had skyrocketed from 11 to 505 in the thirty-five years before the hearing. (The total number of abalone fishermen reached 880 five years later.)

While the fishermen and their supporters continued to hammer away at the economic value of the abalone fishery and their belief in its primacy in the debate, others noted the small number of fishermen who benefitted from the fishery, the aesthetic values of the otters, and the biological value the otters provided to the ecosystem. In the end, however, all agreed that the only solution would be to segregate the otters from the abalone fishing grounds. Yet it prompted Myers to raise a question that would have implications on the resolution of the sea otter debate for the next half century: "If by chance you are successful in moving the sea otter, how would you keep him from coming back down? They are fast swimmers, and they seem to want to go wherever they wish to go."

The senate committee eventually concluded that a sea otter relocation program would be unwise, siding temporarily with the environmental community but leaving unaddressed most of the issues raised by the fishermen, who remained vocal and repeatedly pressed their demands in the political arena. It was a time that Margaret Owings described later as one when "a single fishing boat could come in with 500 pounds of abalone," but "one little otter floating along on its back . . . was all they [the fishermen] needed to see absolute red." In 1967, the state senate passed a resolution reversing its previous conclusion and directed Fish and Game to "determine the feasibility and possible means of confining sea otters within the protection of the existing refuge or other means that will . . . lessen the possibilities of resource conflicts." It was a directive that made the fishermen feel that progress was being made on their behalf, though how it was to be achieved was uncertain. It also motivated sea otter lovers like Owings to take action.

Margaret Owings was a member of the California State Parks Commission and an ardent conservationist who had already spearheaded efforts to prevent the legalized killing of California sea lions, remove a bounty on mountain lions, and divert a highway away from old-growth redwood trees in state parks. After several years of attending meetings of citizen committees and public hearings and being verbally attacked by abalone fishermen, she wrote a letter to the *Monterey Peninsula Herald* in 1968 that was published on the front page under the headline "Do Sea Otters Have Any Friends?" She wrote in her letter that "the return of the otter to the immediate area of our coastal waters has given thousands of visitors a rare pleasure and we, living along the coast, can feel privileged to be able to watch its delightful activities. Yet I am concerned for the welfare of the otter. As has been true with practically every wild animal in the vicinity of man, the otter is thought to compete with an economic value that man claims as his own." She pulled no punches, noting that the population of sea otters had declined in the previous decade and that dead otters were washing ashore with wounds from gunshots and stabbings. She also highlighted the threats from pollution, oil spills, and the fur trade.

Seeing that letter in print galvanized her to start Friends of the Sea Otter, thinking she could probably resolve the issues surrounding the sea otter and the fishermen in "a few years." But it took a few decades longer than that. From its origins at Owings' dining table, and with the help of surgeon James Matteson and with scientific guidance from biologist Jud Vandevere, the leading sea otter biologist of his day, Friends of the Sea Otter grew to five hundred members after its first year, and launched a research program and a group of volunteer "otter watchers" to learn about otter biology and behavior and assist with the state's monthly otter census. Through her sheer force of will, Owings spent decades leading efforts to protect sea otters in California by lobbying politicians in Sacramento and Washington, DC, to establish policies to benefit otters while rallying scientists, conservationists, and the general public to support the cause.

The group initially opposed the relocation of sea otters to preserve the commercial abalone fishery, but that is exactly what the state had in mind. The first step in the state's plan was to remove up to twenty otters from the area off Cambria and Point Estero, where the greatest conflict with fishermen occurred, and relocate them to the northern part of the sea otter refuge or place them in captivity. If that could be accomplished successfully, the relocation of additional otters would be considered. But even finding appropriate relocation sites was difficult. At each of the six proposed sites, conflicts arose from commercial shellfishermen who didn't want sea otters to do to their harvest what the abalone fishermen claimed the otters did to theirs. And initial experiments conducted by Fish and Game to capture and relocate sea otters failed miserably, as the otters either swam right back to their original location or died during the relocation process.

Many minds were changed about the relocation plan, however, when in January 1969 an oil-drilling platform owned by Union Oil ruptured and released one hundred thousand barrels of oil into the Santa Barbara channel. The worst oil-platform spill in US history at that time, it killed thirty-seven thousand seabirds and had a lasting effect on the marine environment in the area. Since no sea otters ranged that far south, none were killed, but it raised alarms among the sea otter conservation community. Margaret Owings and Friends of the Sea Otter imagined the possible extinction of the southern sea otter if an oil spill occurred within the otters' range. Perhaps, they concluded, the establishment of several populations of sea otters through relocation efforts would ensure the animal's survival in the face of a potential future oil spill.

Although reaction to the spill heralded an era of environmental conservation throughout the country, sea otters in California didn't benefit. The election of Ronald Reagan as governor in 1969 and his appointment of Raymond Arnett as the new director of the California Department of Fish and Game led to a reversal in the agency's approach to sea otter conservation. "Fish and Game changed its tune entirely," said Lilian Carswell, the Fish and Wildlife Service biologist charged with managing the recovery plan since the mid-2000s. "Whereas they had been quite protective of sea otters before, they suddenly seemed extremely concerned about the fisheries and way less concerned about otters. The way they put it was, 'We have a secure population of otters here, we're not worried about them, and we just want to keep the rest of the area clear of otters so we can have all the fisheries we want.'"

THE NEW DIRECTION taken by the California government with regard to otters, which was largely in response to the small but vocal group of abalone fishermen, led to a slew of bills and proposals that enraged environmentalists. One bill introduced in the state legislature in 1970 would have required the removal of any otter that wandered outside the sea otter refuge, and the language in the bill suggested that the animals may be killed. Despite the bill's sponsor's backtracking on the controversial language, Friends of the Sea Otter responded with a petition containing fifteen thousand signatures opposing the measure. No vote on the bill was ever taken. While the public response to the bill and other proposals questioned whether Fish and Game's new direction was in the best interest of the public and the state, as the agency claimed, it did not bring about a change in perspective among Fish and Game leadership. Instead, the agency developed a plan for what it called "zonal management," which would create separate geographic regions for sea otters and shellfishing. How that would be achieved was uncertain, in light of the agency's failed relocation experiments.

But the state's plan would never be implemented. The passage of the federal Marine Mammal Protection Act in 1972 and the Endangered Species Act in 1973 saw to that. Those laws didn't stop the fishing industry from promoting its concerns or the conservation community from advocating for its own, but the California Department of Fish and Game no longer had jurisdiction over sea otters. Under the Marine Mammal Protection Act, management authority for sea otters was transferred to the US Fish and Wildlife Service, and California officials weren't happy about it. The state petitioned to retain responsibility for managing its otter populations, but just about everything it proposed was rejected as contrary to the principles of the federal legislation.

The state of California didn't give up; government officials just changed strategies. Instead of requesting that management authority be returned to the state and obtaining a waiver on the moratorium on capturing and killing sea otters, it requested a "scientific research permit" from the Fish and Wildlife Service in 1976 that would enable it to conduct "experimental management procedures" involving the relocation of forty otters from the southern end of their range to the northern end. Knowing full well that the state's objectives were counter to that of the legislation, the California Department of Fish and Game was still issued its research permit.

While all this was happening, the Fish and Wildlife Service added the southern sea otter to the federal endangered species list in 1977, a step that provided an additional level of protection for the species and required a recovery plan be developed. Lilian Carswell said that the plan indicates that sea otters can be considered for removal from the endangered list if their California population reaches 3,090 animals for three consecutive years. Back in 1982, when the plan was first approved, the population had just reached 2,100 and still had a long way to go. The population finally reached the target number for the first time in 2016. Although it would likely be a controversial step to remove sea otters from the endangered list, Carswell doesn't think it would affect the level of protection the animals receive because sea otters would continue to be managed by the Fish and Wildlife Service under the Marine Mammal Protection Act even if they were no longer on the endangered list, and that legislation is even more protective than the Endangered Species Act.

When sea otters were first listed as threatened under the Endangered Species Act, it was due to the small size of the population, its limited range, and its great risk from the increasing offshore oil development taking place nearby. That latter factor led the recovery team to conclude that relocating a number of sea otters to establish a separate population was an "effective and reasonable management action." And the strategy that was eventually endorsed by the federal recovery team was nearly the same one the abalone fishermen had proposed nearly twenty years earlier and which the state Department of Fish and Game had long supported—the establishment of a management zone where sea otters would be excluded, possibly forever. How the otters would be kept out of the zone was, once again, never clearly addressed, and the natural inclination of sea otter males to wander great distances almost ensured the plan would fail, but the plan moved ahead nonetheless.

The idea of zonal management of sea otters was endorsed by the Marine Mammal Commission, an advisory board established by the Marine Mammal Protection Act, in part as a means of separating what it saw as human activities in the marine environment that were incompatible with sea otters. It pointed to commercial gillnet fishing as one such activity that needed to be kept from areas where sea otters lived. About eighty sea otters per year drowned in gillnets from 1982 to 1984, and many more were rumored to have died in previous years. So the fishery's manager, Fish and Game, established a series of regulations that pushed the gillnet fishery into zones far enough offshore that it no longer affected the otters. Since zonal management appeared to work in that case, it was argued, it should work with the incompatible abalone fishery, too.

The relocation site that was selected was San Nicolas Island, the most remote of the Channel Islands, an uninhabited island located ninety-one miles southwest of Los Angeles that is controlled by the US Navy for use in weapons testing and training. It was a site that Friends of the Sea Otter had long considered a suitable place for establishing a new population of sea otters, far enough distant from the existing range that both populations would not likely be affected by a single oil spill. And because the island had an abundance of food and was located a great distance from the mainland across a deep ocean channel, many biologists believed the animals would not try to swim back to the mainland. They were wrong.

Before the plan went forward, however, the fishermen pushed for even more concessions, as did the oil and gas industry and the US Navy. Perhaps the most challenging concession, which was codified in a federal law signed by President Ronald Reagan in 1986, required that any sea otter from either the coastal range or the San Nicolas Island population that strayed into the management zone designated for shellfisheries would be removed by "all feasible nonlethal means." That stipulation would eventually be the plan's undoing.

Finally, in 1987, after more than a decade of haggling over the details, the plan was approved. It established what came to be known as a "no-otter zone" southward from Point Conception, a headland that is commonly used as the dividing line between central and Southern California. No sea otters were to be allowed anywhere south of that point, except in the relocation zone around San Nicolas Island. Since the southern extent of the sea otters' range was not far from Point Conception already, those involved knew it wouldn't be long before natural range expansion would push them into the no-otter zone. But problems emerged long before that happened.

As biologists—and even many fishermen—had been saying for twenty-five years, it's impossible to keep a sea otter somewhere in the marine environment that it doesn't want to be. And that proved to be the case in California. Just as had happened in all of the experimental relocation efforts in the years prior, most of the 140 sea otters that were captured and brought to San Nicolas Island from 1987 to 1991 departed the region almost immediately or simply disappeared. "They were leaving almost as fast as they were brought there," Carswell said. "Some juveniles stayed around a little while, so people got encouraged by that, but eventually they left, too. They just grew up a little first." Some never even made it to the island. Carswell heard that four older males appeared to die of heart attacks from the stress of the capture and relocation process. All otters that made it to the island were tagged so they could be monitored, but many were never seen again. "Many of those probably died, but their bodies were never found, so no one knows exactly what happened," said Carswell. "They might have slipped back into the central coast range undetected, but probably a lot of them were panicked, they didn't know where they were, they swam off into the ocean, and they died." The fate of only half of the animals is known. Some quickly returned to the exact place on the central coast where they were first captured. Others detoured to unexpected locations: about twenty found their way seventy-four miles north to San Miguel Island, where they may have established a new colony, but because it was located in the no-otter zone, they were captured again and removed.

By 1993, the recovery team suspended its efforts to remove otters from the no-otter zone so it could reevaluate its methods. By then, however, because just a dozen sea otters remained at San Nicolas Island and almost no otters were wandering into the no-otter zone, learning new methods of capturing and relocating sea otters was no longer a priority. Five years later, the southward expansion of their range resulted in large numbers of sea otters entering the management zone, renewing calls by fishermen for the animals' removal. Although the idea behind the no-otter zone was to contain the relocated population of otters to San Nicolas Island rather than to put a halt to range expansion, the management plan did not make that distinction, further infuriating the fishermen when the Fish and Wildlife Service made no effort to remove the expanding otters from the zone. In 2001, the service issued a new policy indicating that removal of otters from the no-otter zone was inconsistent with the Endangered Species Act, and no further action would be taken until the management plan was reevaluated. A new recovery plan for the southern sea otter was issued two years later and recommended that sea otters should be allowed to naturally expand their range to further the species' recovery. And the recovery team advised that the management zone concept was a failure and should be discontinued. It took more than a decade—as well as lawsuits from both environmentalists and fishermen and more than twenty-seven thousand comments from the public—but the no-otter zone was officially declared invalid in December 2012, and sea otters were allowed to continue their range expansion unabated.

The fishermen remained unhappy, however, preferring a failed otter containment program to none at all, but by then their issues had changed. Commercial abalone fishing had come to an end in California in 1997, and the reasons had little to do with sea otters. Abalone had been subject to what some have described as serial depletion—after fishermen depleted the easiest-to-access and most desirable species, they moved on to the next species and then the next until there were few abalone of any variety left. That meant that the species living in the deepest water and those that were never particularly abundant were targeted last. That last species, the white abalone, which is found in water eighty to two hundred feet deep, was wiped out in just six years of fishing. By 1996 white abalone populations had declined by 99 percent, and five years later the white abalone was added to the federal endangered species list. It became the first marine invertebrate to be listed as endangered, and today the National Marine Fisheries Service considers it almost biologically extinct. Despite claims by many fishermen that sea otters were to blame, most agree that sea otters had no role in the white abalone's decline, since its range and the range of the sea otter do not overlap.

All that remains of the abalone fishery today is a small sport fishery north of San Francisco that requires breath-hold diving only and a daily bag limit of three red abalone. The fishermen saw the approaching end of the commercial fishery as long ago as the 1980s, and many of them switched to harvesting sea urchins. Urchins, the spiny globular creatures that some say look like underwater hedgehogs, were promoted by the National Marine Fisheries Service as an underutilized resource that was depleting kelp beds and destroying fish habitat in areas where sea otters were absent. Today it's the urchin fishermen who are the most vocal group opposed to the range expansion of sea otters in California. Sea urchins are often considered a sea otter's favorite food, and the hungry otters can easily outcompete the fishermen for their catch. But the sea otters' range does not yet overlap with the urchin-fishing grounds in southern California, so there is no direct competition. Yet the fishermen are rightly worried that otters will move into their favorite fishing areas if nothing is done to stop them. So they continue to file and appeal lawsuits and introduce legislation to reinstate the no-otter zone, so far with little success.

As more and more time passes, however, public support for sea otters continues to grow. It is driving the economy in Monterey and nearby Moss Landing, and it's a major component of the economy in Morro Bay and many communities in between. A 2005 economic analysis claimed that the economic benefits of allowing sea otters to expand their range southward into Santa Barbara County could top $100 million annually, even when factoring in commercial fishing losses. While that report has been much criticized, anecdotal evidence suggests that there are plenty more people benefitting economically from sea otter watching than ever participated in the abalone or urchin fisheries. "You can see it clearly within the sea otter range that kayak and ecotourism companies are benefitting a lot from having sea otters there," Carswell said.

So while the controversy caused by the repopulation of sea otters in California isn't entirely in the past, it's clear that opposition is waning. In locations where otters have long become reestablished, like Monterey Bay, controversy has given way to adulation. The healthy otter populations there have made Monterey sea otters the most studied and best-understood sea otters in the world. And yet their use as wild research subjects is far from over.

Chapter 3: Catch and Release

MONTEREY, CALIFORNIA

THE WATERFRONT in Monterey, California, is a bustling place, with boats of many sizes and varieties scattered among its three public wharfs, where an abundance of shopping and dining establishments mix with street performers, fishermen, and tourists. Perched on the southern edge of Monterey Bay, a two-hour drive south of San Francisco, the city is renowned for its annual jazz festival, year-round whale-watching cruises, a highly respected and well-funded aquarium, and a history made famous by novelist John Steinbeck, who grew up in nearby Salinas and whose colorful novel of the city's waning days as the West Coast sardine-canning capital earned him a Nobel Prize. In *Cannery Row*, Steinbeck described the infamous street in 1930s Monterey as "a poem, a stink, a grating noise, a quality of light, a tone, a habit, a nostalgia, a dream. Cannery Row is the gathered and scattered, tin and iron and rust and splintered wood, chipped pavement and weedy lots and junk heaps, sardine canneries of corrugated iron, honky-tonks, restaurants and whorehouses, and little crowded groceries, and laboratories and flophouses."

It has changed a great deal since then. Now a major tourist destination, it retains some of its historic cannery buildings, though they have now been turned into boutique hotels and trinket shops. The major draw for me, however, lies right behind the waterfront buildings—perhaps the most productive kelp forests in the state. That's where Renay and I were headed to get our first hands-on encounter with sea otters.

Coast Guard Pier, located at the entrance to Cannery Row, is home to dozens of commercial and recreational boats, Monterey Bay National Marine Sanctuary vessels, and, of course, the Coast Guard. It's also home to hundreds of California sea lions that line the piers and breakwater, barking and fighting and resting and making the area smell like a cesspool when the wind blows just the right way. They are usually joined by a few harbor seals and, infrequently, an elephant seal. At eight thirty on a late September morning, we met a team of ten biologists, interns, and volunteers to discuss the logistics of capturing live sea otters in the nearby waters and delivering them to the Monterey Bay Aquarium to be implanted with tracking devices. Six members of the team were designated as shore spotters, who spread out at several sites where otters were commonly observed and spent the day watching through high-powered telescopes for groups of resting otters that could potentially be captured.

Renay and I joined otter biologist Tim Tinker and divers Joe Tomoleoni and Mike Kenner on a gray, twenty-foot Boston Whaler named *Pursuit*, which was loaded with dive gear, Wilson traps, and safety equipment. The traps consist of a simple net inside a circular metal frame that is pushed up from below a resting sea otter. A manual drawstring closes the net when an otter is inside. It sounds simple, but as we soon learned, it is a complex process to capture live sea otters in the wild, one that requires a great deal of waiting and watching, sneaky strategy, and plenty of luck. And at any time, a wayward kayaker, sea lion, or piece of kelp can lead to failure.

After a very short ride—no more than a half mile from the pier to the opposite end of Cannery Row—Tinker turned off the engine and we drifted just offshore of the aquarium. The entire area is an immense kelp bed, from the harbor out and around the Monterey peninsula and extending almost a quarter mile from shore. The upper reaches of giant kelp were massed at the surface of the water everywhere, and marine life was abundant. As we looked down into the glassy water, it appeared as if we were peering down from the canopy of a liquid forest, which we sort of were. Great egrets and double-crested cormorants perched warily on some of the sturdier branches, while sea lions and seals repeatedly surfaced unexpectedly in all directions. Almost everywhere we turned, long chains of salps—tiny jellyfish-like creatures that look somewhat like clear caterpillars—were visible an arm's reach below the surface. Occasionally we saw a school of herring or a small salmon darting by, and solitary kelp rockfish could often be seen pausing motionless for long minutes at a time, as if they thought they were well camouflaged. They weren't.

We pulled up to the retractable pier at the aquarium to pick up a four-foot wooden crate to hold captured otters on the boat, and then we cruised slowly a couple hundred yards toward a rocky outcrop at Stanford University's Hopkins Marine Station. The rocks there were covered with three varieties of cormorants, brown pelicans, and a few harbor seals, but it was the sea otters just beyond the rocks that caught our attention. It's a common hangout location for otters, so as we approached the area, Tinker quietly called on the radio to the nearby spotters to determine whether any otters were resting there and could be targeted for capture. The calm voice from shore reported that three otters had been resting together for some time, so we stopped about one hundred yards from the otters and tied the boat to a handful of kelp to wait and watch. We were much closer to the otters than is typical at any other otter-trapping site in California, because the Monterey otters are used to seeing boaters and kayakers nearby and are less likely to become spooked and dive.

As Tomoleoni and Kenner prepared to get in the water, a kayaker and paddleboarder glided near the otters, causing one of the animals to awaken and dive. It was an issue that would plague us all day. But with two otters still resting, the divers prepared their dry suits and other gear, including what they called scooters, which they use to propel themselves through the water. Looking like a small industrial fan, a scooter is held with two hands and pulls the diver smoothly through the water. The trap is attached to the front of the scooter so when the divers are about ten or fifteen feet below the otters, they can rapidly propel themselves upward to capture the otters.

We continued to watch the otters, all of which were now wrapped in kelp and resting. The researchers don't even attempt to capture otters that are actively grooming or foraging, because the animals will be more aware of the divers approaching, so we waited to make sure they were settled down completely. Two of the otters already had tags attached to their flippers, indicating that they had previously been captured and might be particularly wary of the boat and divers. As we waited, we sat low in the boat and whispered so as not to raise the alert level of the otters, but none of the other wildlife in the area followed our lead. A Pacific bottlenose dolphin surfaced near the otters, dived below them, and resurfaced again before disappearing. Harbor seals and cormorants appeared and disappeared as well, gulls cried out loudly, and sea lions barked in the distance, but the sea otters appeared oblivious to it all. So the divers slid overboard and waited for Tinker to hand each of them a scooter and trap. As they descended silently beneath the surface and propelled themselves away from the boat, they reminded me of the underwater chase scenes from an early James Bond movie.

As planned, Tomoleoni briefly surfaced halfway between the boat and the otters. It allowed him to get a picture of the exact location of the otters, and it allowed the antenna of a radio attached to the headpiece of his dive suit to rise above the waterline, enabling Tinker to radio him and tell him the status of the otters and any other necessary information. Tomoleoni surfaced one more time even closer to the otters before disappearing for good. Tinker said that it is sometimes difficult to tell whether it is a diver surfacing or a harbor seal, so he sometimes gives instructions over the radio to a seal, thinking it's Tomoleoni.

We then stared through our binoculars at the otters, not knowing exactly when the divers would breach the surface with their traps and set into motion an hour of hasty activities. As our arms became sore from holding our binoculars to our eyes, we wondered aloud about the delay. Had the divers lost sight of the otters? Were they tangled in kelp? What could provoke that five-minute delay? And then we saw the splash.

For the divers, timing is everything. If they reach the surface simultaneously, they have a better chance of capturing two otters, whereas a delay by one diver—even a slight one—makes it likely that the second otter will be alerted in time to escape. Which is exactly what happened. Kenner's trap appeared at the surface first, and although the splash obscured my ability to tell how it happened, he succeeded in capturing his targeted otter. But Tomoleoni was a split second behind Kenner, and while it appeared to me that Tomoleoni's otter leapt up and landed in his trap, the animal actually leapt away and escaped. The wave of one diver's hand—I couldn't tell who it was—signaled that the boat could approach, so Tinker pulled the *Pursuit* alongside the divers to retrieve the captured sea otter.

It was immediately obvious that the otter wasn't happy. At the side of the boat, it hissed and fought aggressively to escape, repeatedly biting on the trap's metal frame, attempting to push through the netting, and continuously spinning and trying to dive. Its efforts were fruitless. But it was the closest I had ever come to a wild otter, so although I felt bad for the unhappy animal, the moment was also quite exciting. Tinker identified it as a young female, which we would later learn was pregnant. She was an attractive chocolate brown with no apparent injuries or other concerns. Tinker and the divers lifted the trap from the water, set it over the open crate, and released the drawstring from the net; the otter dropped into the crate. I quickly closed the crate door, and we had our first otter securely stowed.

I asked the divers what went on beneath the surface during the capture process, and Tomoleoni said his scooter was wobbling throughout the dive, providing him with less than half the normal power output. That meant that he didn't have enough speed to push through the kelp and keep up with Kenner as they surfaced together. Visibility was great, he said, but the large quantity of kelp the otters were resting on and his scooter's power deficiency made it impossible for him to break through the obstructions to capture his otter. Kenner, on the other hand, called his experience "textbook" because it required only a short swim to the otters, he could see the animals well, and he captured his target. At most other sites, the divers have to swim more than three hundred yards through thick kelp and swells to reach the otters, so this one was easy by comparison.

"This was like nursery school, it was so easy," Tinker said. And besides, added Kenner, "the reflections off all of the salps in the water made the swim feel like I was in *Star Wars.*"

After a short run to the aquarium pier, we unloaded the otter-filled crate into the hands of a team of veterinary assistants and took on an empty crate.

THE LIVE SEA OTTERS captured that day are part of a long-term monitoring program led by Tinker and his predecessors. The veterinary team collects a comprehensive series of health measurements, similar to routine exams done on dogs, cats, and humans, after which the otters are implanted with a tracking device and released back into the wild. From that day forward, every tracked otter is monitored every single day for several years by a team of biologists and volunteers to learn about its movement patterns, social interactions, behavior, diet, and reproductive success. Combined with annual population surveys and mortality data collected from otters found dead on the shore, this record of daily sightings and activities provides tremendous insight into the lives and health of sea otters in California. Tinker said that none of the three data sets is particularly useful on its own, but putting them all together "is the most powerful thing that we do." Many of the otters will eventually be recaptured sometime in the future, allowing the researchers to compare changes in the animals' health. By knowing what the animals did from day to day, where they lived, and what they ate between captures, Tinker's team is able to pinpoint the factors that affect each otter's health and create a picture of the overall health of the otters in different parts of the state.

"The big picture is that this longitudinal data on individual animals provides us insight into what drives the population and how sea otters as apex predators are interacting with all of the other species here to affect ecosystem dynamics," he said. "Without this monitoring data, what we'd know about sea otters, very optimistically, would be one-tenth of what we know today, and probably a lot less."

He admitted that it will probably take years before he learns much from the otters we captured that day. But each animal is likely to eventually provide important insights that will help ensure the long-term survival of the species. And the ongoing monitoring activity and health data provide opportunities for many smaller research projects, like studies of territorial behaviors, reproductive success, or genetics.

AFTER RETURNING to the marina to fix Tomoleoni's scooter, Tinker had a quick conversation on the radio with the spotters, and we headed a short distance away to the waters off the Monterey Bay Inn, where another group of resting sea otters awaited us. We could see the spotters watching from the deck of the inn as we maneuvered around a dead sea lion floating on a sturdy stalk of kelp and got into position for the next dive. For several minutes, we watched four resting otters—two wrapped quietly in kelp and two somewhat actively grooming and looking around. As we waited for them to settle, kayakers came very close to the otters, so close that Tinker said they were breaking federal law for disturbing marine mammals. We worried that the kayakers would startle the otters and we would have to abandon the effort, but the otters remained calm and the divers slid into the water. This time, however, the otters were amid a thicker forest of kelp, making it difficult for the divers to see the animals from underwater. After another long wait, Tomoleoni and Kenner retreated briefly to get another look at the otters from the surface, then moved in. With another big splash, they caught two animals.

When we delivered the first of the two sea otters to the aquarium dock, Renay and I climbed off the boat and followed the crate up a freight elevator and into the animal health laboratory, where veterinarian Mike Murray and six assistants and onlookers crowded around a small stainless-steel table that was ready to receive the otter. The room looked like a fancy version of the vet's office where I take my cats—glass-fronted cabinets containing drugs and supplies, a table for the "patient," and a high-tech scale. When the crate was opened, Murray, decked out in jelly-bean scrubs and a trim gray beard, grabbed the otter's flipper while an assistant injected an anesthesia cocktail into the animal's thigh. Then the crate was closed again for several minutes to let the drugs take effect. After lifting the limp animal onto the table, the assemblage collected measurements that were called out and written on a data sheet—weight, 34.1 kilograms; length, 134.4 centimeters; girth, 81.3 centimeters; canine tooth, 8.4 centimeters; tail, 31.9 centimeters; scapula, 17.4 centimeters; body temperature, 100.9 degrees Fahrenheit; respiration, 16 breaths per minute; heart rate, 130 beats per minute. After peering into the otter's mouth, Murray added, "It also has a great personality and a fine sense of humor." The otter was estimated to be eleven years old, based on his grizzled appearance and the condition of his cracked, worn, and broken teeth.

Then an oxygen mask was placed over the otter's head, and bags of ice were placed on his chest, under his arms, and on his crotch and flippers to keep him cool. Several vials of blood were collected from his jugular vein while Murray collected a smaller sample from a vein in the otter's leg to test the animal's blood glucose level—94 milligrams. Next a tube was placed down the otter's throat and attached to a ventilator. When the oxygen hood was removed so the otter could be transported into the surgical ward, the hood was filled with tiny nasal mites that had escaped from the animal's nose. "Tastes just like chicken," said a smiling Murray.

THE TRANSMITTERS implanted into the sea otters we captured are the size of a small bar of soap and have been the primary technology used to track a wide range of animal species for close to thirty years. The device consists of a clear resin block containing three small batteries, an antenna, and an electronic device that transmits a pinging sound over a particular radio frequency that can be detected by a receiver aboard a boat. It collects no data. Instead, it transmits the signal to identify the animal's precise location, somewhat like the GPS feature in many cars and cell phones. According to Zach Randell, a doctoral student at the University of California, Santa Cruz, who works with Tinker, the transmitter is temperature dependent. It broadcasts a signal twice every minute if the animal is alive and maintaining its normal body temperature, and one beat per minute if the animal is dead and cold. Dead animals are retrieved for studies of their body condition, health, and cause of death.

Some animals—though not those we captured that day—are also implanted with a device called a time and depth recorder, or TDR. It is a cylindrical piece of plastic a little larger than a cigarette that records how deep the animal is in the water every second. When recovered from the otter, it provides data that shows how often and how deep the animal dives below the surface of the water. "Between the TDR and observational data from our volunteers, we get a lot of data that can tell us exactly what each otter was doing from minute to minute every day," Randell said.

The process of implanting the $800 transmitter into the otter we delivered to the aquarium began with a sterile lubricant being spread on its belly and combed in, allowing the surgical assistant to separate the fur and find the animal's naval, where the incision would begin. Murray then entered the room in full surgical garb, and everyone became quiet. Only the sound of the beeping heart monitor could be heard. He made a four-inch incision and carefully cut through skin and muscle to make a small hole in the body cavity. In one quick motion, he grabbed the transmitter, slid it into the hole, and began to suture the incision. "I suppose I could have made it more exciting, but that's really all there is to it," he said. The longest part of the entire process was the suturing, which he did in four layers. "We don't want him to come unzipped." If it's not closed well, his skin won't be well protected from the cold. "Suturing well helps me sleep at night," Murray said.

During the surgery, a nurse collected nasal swabs and fur samples, while biologist Michelle Staedler punched a tiny hole in the skin between toes four and five of his left flipper and attached tag number 6300. She repeated the process on the right flipper with tag number 6987. The location of the right flipper tag identifies the animal's gender—between toes four and five for males, between toes one and two for females. The color of the tag indicates to the scientists which research project the otter is involved in or where the otter lives. The plug of skin tissue removed for the tag was saved for later DNA analysis. A passive integrated transponder, or PIT tag, an electronic device the size of a grain of rice that is commonly used to identify domestic dogs and cats, was also injected into the animal's leg. The entire surgical procedure took no more than twenty minutes.

The otter was then placed back in the crate, given a shot to reverse the anesthetic, and within thirty seconds was awake and ready for release. Back aboard the boat, we drove to the same spot where we had captured the sea otter, set the crate on the edge of the boat, and opened the door. The otter slowly climbed out, looked over his shoulder at us, and swam away. He resurfaced next to what we believe was the same group of animals he had been resting with prior to capture, as if nothing had happened.

WE THEN RETURNED to an area just east of the aquarium, in front of a new hotel, where two otters were resting in the kelp one hundred yards offshore. The divers prepped their gear, and we again waited to ensure the otters remained calm. Once again, however, a kayaker drifted too close, and although the otters initially looked like they were going to sit still, they slowly rolled over and dived.

So we moved a bit to another group of three otters that the spotters said had been resting quietly for more than an hour. After only a brief period of waiting, the divers slipped into the water and captured one of the two otters they targeted. Again, Kenner hit the surface first and successfully captured a young female otter, but Tomoleoni's targeted animal leapt upward and away from the trap. We dropped off the newly captured otter at the aquarium and picked up the previous female for release. When the crate was opened, she slid out quickly, dived deep, then surfaced twenty yards away without looking back.

We repeated the process one more time back where the kayaker had disturbed the group of otters an hour previously, and the divers succeeded in capturing two more animals to finish out the day's activity just as the sun was dipping beneath the horizon. It had been a very long day, but with six otters captured, Tinker considered it a tremendous success.

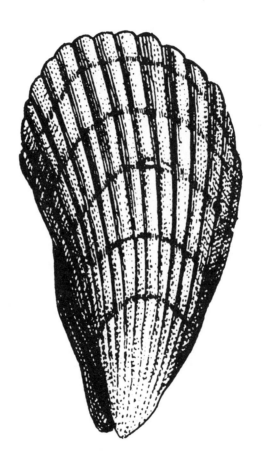

Chapter 4: Shifting Paradigm

LIKE EVERY one of the two dozen sea otter researchers I've met, Tim Tinker didn't start out with any particular passion for studying sea otters. He grew up in Ontario and earned a master's degree studying gray seals in the Gulf of Saint Lawrence. At a marine mammal conference in Texas in the early 1990s, he met Jim Estes, whose early investigations of sea otter ecology are the foundation of nearly every sea otter study in recent decades. During the conference, Estes recruited Tinker to help him study sea otters in the Aleutian Islands, and a week later Tinker was dropped off on Amchitka Island for four months. Tinker was the right man for the job: he was interested in ecology, enjoyed studying animal behavior and population biology, and wasn't averse to conducting remote fieldwork. When he completed his stint on Amchitka Island, Estes offered him another year of sea otter work in the Aleutians, beginning a long-term working relationship that continues today.

The first thing I learned about Tinker, well before I observed him trap otters on the *Pursuit*, is that he is a hard man to reach. It took me a few months. But when I finally tracked him down at a meeting in Alaska, he remembered my messages and could not have been more generous with his time. The other thing I learned about Tinker—this time from his fellow sea otter researchers—is that he makes their heads hurt. That's because his expertise at

---

creating and interpreting complex computer models is way over the heads of nearly everyone with whom he works. I understood their predicament when I first sat down to speak with him. I'm still not sure I understand some of what he said.

Tinker's research takes place everywhere and anywhere sea otters are found, including Russia, the Aleutian Islands, Prince William Sound, Southeast Alaska, British Columbia, and especially California. But his home base is the Long Marine Laboratory at the University of California, Santa Cruz, which doubles as the Santa Cruz Field Station of the US Geological Survey's Western Ecological Research Center and has become the world's capital of sea otter research over the last forty years. Nearly every sea otter biologist I met had a connection to the university, either as a professor, graduate student, or alumnus. It seems that everyone who wants to study sea otters eventually finds their way to Santa Cruz.

When I finally sat down to talk with Tinker in his office, he half smiled at me and said, "I'm kind of evil." It was his way of explaining that he is not like those at aquariums who rescue stranded sea otters and care for them for months at a time. He's also not like the pathologists who examine every dead sea otter to determine its cause of death. "I don't really care about the fate of individuals. I look at the really big picture of things. I'm looking at what makes an entire population grow at the rate it does."

Unfortunately, the sea otter population in California has been growing very slowly. And that has been the main problem that Tinker and Estes and many other sea otter biologists have been worrying about for many years. They were certain that something was happening in the population to keep their numbers down, but years and years of study could not uncover what was causing the slow growth. In Southeast Alaska, the sea otter population grew at more than 15 percent per year for fifty years after they were reintroduced to the region in the 1960s. But in California, the growth rate has been just 5 percent per year since the 1930s, and lately the population has barely grown at all. The scientists compared California birth rates and mortality rates and any number of other issues with the comparable rates in Alaska, Washington, and British Columbia, where growth rates topped out at 20 percent in some years, but never did they identify a cause for California's slow growth. Yet they continued to seek answers.

The results of the 2016 survey of sea otters in California found 3,272 otters, including nearly one hundred animals at San Nicholas Island, with the remainder along the central coast bounded by Point Conception in the south and Half Moon Bay in the north. The problem is clearly not at San Nicholas Island, where sea otter numbers have increased annually by 16 percent in recent years. Food is abundant there, and where food is abundant, populations can grow quickly. Because the island is small, however, Tinker anticipates that the San Nicholas Island population growth will begin to slow soon after the abundant and easy-to-access food becomes depleted. But he's not worried about what is happening there. The big worry has been the mainland population, where there has been no measurable growth over the last five to seven years. About 80 percent of all southern sea otters are found in the central part of the coastal range, between the northern edge of the Monterey peninsula and the resort community of Cayucos, just north of Morro Bay. The otter population is quite dense along that 115-mile stretch, yet it hasn't grown in twenty-five years.

"That population is at dynamic equilibrium," said Tinker. "You might get a couple of very productive years and it will go up a bit, but then you'll get less productive years and it will go down a bit.

It's at carrying capacity." That means that given the food and habitat available, the environment in that stretch of coastline already has the maximum number of otters it can sustain. And in this particular case, the limiting factor is food. There isn't enough food available there to provide for a larger population of sea otters. And as a result, it is virtually impossible for the otter population to grow there. Even if it were possible to remove some of the sources of mortality, like disease or boat strikes, the otters would die of something else because there just isn't enough food to sustain them.

However, at the northern and southern extremes of their range, where otters have only recently begun to recolonize, they are found in lower densities and food is relatively abundant. "What ultimately limits sea otters in a given area is their prey," Tinker said. "That's the definition of an apex predator. They're not limited by animals above them on the food chain. They're limited by the trophic levels below them."

While the otter population had experienced strong growth at the edges of its coastal range as the animals expanded into new areas, that growth stopped in the early 2000s. That's when mortality from shark bites skyrocketed in those two regions, limiting range expansion to the north and south and eliminating population growth in the only parts of the coastal range where population growth was even possible. According to Tinker, there has always been a high level of shark-bite mortality in the northern part of the sea otter range between Santa Cruz and Half Moon Bay because large numbers of great white sharks are attracted to nearby Año Nuevo Island to feed on the massive herd of elephant seals that congregates there each winter. That area had typically been a region dominated by male sea otters, so while otter mortality from sharks slowed overall population growth, it didn't have a significant effect on long-term population trends, since few females were killed there. It's the females that drive range expansion and population growth. But when shark-bite mortality increased at the southern end of the range, where both males and females were being killed, otter numbers began trending downward. Tinker described it as "a new nucleus of shark mortality" that began near Pismo Beach and expanded from there. Whereas the population in the southern third of the otters' range had previously been growing at 5 to 6 percent per year, it began declining at 2 percent per year after 2005, with nearly 70 percent of all otter deaths in the region caused by sharks. Tinker said the sea otters in the area of the Santa Barbara Channel were big and healthy, reproductive success was high, and food was abundant. If it weren't for the sharks, that area could have grown at rates comparable to San Nicholas Island, fueling growth in the statewide population despite the no-growth region in the middle part of the range. "Right now there's a 30 percent chance that an otter of any age in any one year is going to die from a shark bite," Tinker said. "That's just too high. When you have that level of risk from one source of mortality, you cannot really sustain population growth."

UNFORTUNATELY, there is little that can be done about shark-bite mortality. Like sea otters, great white sharks are protected in California waters, and no one really has any idea how many white sharks even live there. Unlike sea otters, which spend much of their lives at the surface of the water, sharks never need to surface, so counting them is extremely difficult. But Chris Lowe, director of the shark lab at California State University in Long Beach, is convinced that great white shark numbers are increasing. At nursery areas in Southern California, he has observed a steady increase in baby white sharks over the last ten to fifteen years. He thinks that a 1994 law banning gillnet fishing within three miles of shore has reduced the number of sharks killed by commercial fishermen and is boosting the overall population. He also thinks improved water quality and improved management of coastal fisheries have led to more fish being available as prey for juvenile sharks as well as for seals and sea lions, whose populations have exploded since the 1970s.

Does this purported white shark population growth explain why so many sea otters are being killed by sharks? Maybe. Lowe says one hypothesis is that the increasing number of subadult sharks—those that have reached nine feet in length—begin to realize that they can prey on larger animals than the flatfish and stingrays they ate as juveniles. In their naïveté, they take a bite of a sea otter. It may also be that otters are wandering farther offshore in search of food, making them more accessible to adult sharks. Or perhaps it's adult sharks moving back to their preferred feeding grounds closer to shore after human conflicts had previously pushed them away from the coast. No one really knows which it is, or if it's something else entirely.

Perhaps worst of all, however, is that the sharks don't even consume the otters. Rather than gaining the abundant nutrition from eating otters, the sharks just chomp down on them—Tinker called it "taking a taste"—and spit them out. "We've never seen a partially eaten sea otter, and no white shark biologist has ever found otter remains in a white shark," explained Tinker. "It looks like they're just taking a single bite. We have thousands of otter carcasses that have been bitten by sharks, and there's never been any tissue missing. It's always a single bite." Presumably, the sharks bite the otters to determine whether they are something the sharks want to eat, like a seal, and after that first bite the sharks decide they don't want any more. A population of white sharks apparently does the same thing to seabirds in Australia. In the case of sea otters, the animals end up with a semicircular pattern of puncture wounds on both sides of their body. The sharks also leave scrapes along otter bones—telltale markings from their serrated teeth—and occasionally chips of shark teeth are found in otter carcasses. Both confirm to pathologists that great white sharks, and not another species, caused the damage. If the otter does not die immediately from acute trauma, it dies days or weeks later of an internal infection as a result of seawater entering the body cavity through the punctures. Several sea otters implanted with data recorders have been bitten by sharks, and when the data was retrieved, it showed that at the moment the animals were bitten, they experienced an instantaneous drop of four degrees in body temperature. Most probably went into shock and died as their core temperature continued to plummet.

So without any other options, Tinker said the best that can be done about the increase in shark-bite mortality is to keep an eye on it and try to learn from it. No one in the marine-science world would advance a plan to control or reduce the population of great white sharks to protect sea otters, even if it were legal and possible. And there is no way to keep the otters from areas where sharks are known to feed. So even though sharks are now the leading cause of death among otters at the northern and southern ends of their range in California, Tinker said the focus of sea otter conservation should still be on understanding and reducing the sources of mortality that can be controlled, like boat strikes, pollutants, and pathogens caused by human activities. "That's not going to solve the shark problem," he said, "but it will certainly mitigate the overall level of mortality."

Chris Lowe agrees. It would be a different story if one of the animals were an invasive species, but a native shark preying upon a native otter is entirely natural. "There may be some losers in this situation, but every time humans try to intervene in these kinds of situations, we really screw things up," he said. "These animals have been coexisting for millions of years, so my guess is that the sea otters will eventually get smarter." That's assuming that limited food resources don't put them further at risk.

THE PHENOMENA of shark-bite mortality at the edges of the sea otter's range and food limitation in the middle of the range are relatively recent explanations for the lack of growth in the otter population in California. But growth was slow long before those issues came to the fore. For almost their entire careers Tinker and Estes have been trying to understand why that has happened, and they think they finally know. They describe their conclusion as a paradigm shift in the way they think about how and why populations grow. But it's not a particularly satisfying answer to those of us who love to solve mysteries. The answer, they now say, is that the population hasn't been growing slowly after all; it has been growing at the speed at which it is supposed to grow.

According to Tinker, there was never a problem with the California population of sea otters. Nothing out of the ordinary was happening to them to keep their numbers low when compared to otters in other regions. Despite years of detective work, there was never really a mystery that needed solving. The tool that the scientific community needed to understand the situation was the science of spatial ecology. That's because the reason California growth rates are so much lower than elsewhere has everything to do with the space the otters are living in. After fifteen years of intensive monitoring of individual sea otters in California and Alaska, Tinker found that survival rates and growth rates were similar if he assumed that habitat and food availability were similar, too. But they are not.

If you imagine a map of the central coast of California, from San Francisco south to Santa Barbara, it's a long, somewhat straight line with habitat for sea otters extending only a couple hundred yards offshore. Compare that to Southeast Alaska, including the 1,100 islands of the Alexander Archipelago, and you'll see why space is so important to understanding sea otter growth rates. Although the linear distances—as the crow flies—are quite similar in California and Southeast Alaska, the space available for sea otters to live in Alaska is many times greater because of all the habitat bordering the islands and bays and inlets that make up its geography. Tinker describes the space for the otter population in California as a long, narrow thread of habitat compared to the sponge of Southeast Alaska.

"So when sea otters are expanding along this thread of habitat," he said, "very quickly most of the otters are going to be stuck in the middle and the only areas where it's going to be growing are the two ends of the thread. But when you're growing in a sponge like Southeast Alaska, it's actually spreading in all directions." In addition, the sea otters in California started from one small group in Big Sur, while those in Alaska started from six small groups relocated from the Aleutian Islands. "If you think of it like a paper towel and you're dropping water at six different locations, it's going to spread over that whole paper towel really fast. In California, though, you have a really long, narrow thread of paper towel, and when you drop just one spot of water in the middle, it's going to spread very slowly north and south. The otters in any one place are no sicker or poorer, they have babies at the same rate, they live and die at the same rate. It's just that in California they quickly reach carrying capacity, and in Alaska it's still a growing population."

When Tinker plugged a bunch of habitat maps and numbers into his complicated computer model, beginning with one hundred sea otters in California in 1938, the model concluded that in seventy-five years there should be three thousand otters in California. Which there are. And when he did the same thing for Southeast Alaska beginning with the numbers from 1964, when the animals were relocated there, the model indicated that there should be twenty thousand otters after forty years. And that's about right, too.

There is only one way to make the California population of sea otters grow at rates approaching those in Southeast Alaska, he said. And that would be to establish additional new populations at other sites along the coastline that do not presently have any sea otters. The California population would have grown in a similar fashion to Southeast Alaska's if it had started from multiple populations like the Southeast Alaska population did. And it still could, if a decision were made to introduce additional populations in Northern and Southern California. "In the first ten years you wouldn't see any difference, but over fifty years you will end up with twice as many otters as you would otherwise," Tinker said.

AS TINKER CONTINUES to fine-tune his research into the population dynamics of sea otters, one of his doctoral students is investigating their little-known sensory system. Sarah McKay Strobel said that sea otters don't appear to see or hear or smell much better than most other marine mammals or their close relatives in the

Mustelidae family, but their tremendous efficiency at finding the enormous quantity of food their metabolism requires every day suggests that they have unique abilities that may be as yet undiscovered. Although the animals are relatively easy to observe and study at the surface, what they do underwater and how exactly they detect and find food is uncertain. Strobel studied the sensory systems of fish as an undergraduate, and she hopes she can use that experience to identify how sea otters sense their environment. "The world only exists in the way we sense it," she said. "Humans are biased toward the visual, but sea otters may sense the world very differently."

Strobel is hoping that a captive sea otter named Selka, formerly known at the Monterey Bay Aquarium as Otter 595, will provide the answers she seeks. Selka became separated from her mother and stranded on a beach when she was just one week old, in July 2012. She was raised for several months by two surrogate mothers at the aquarium—the first of which died suddenly of a brain tumor before Selka was weaned—and it was later determined that Selka could not be released back into the wild. So she was introduced to Strobel and is living in captivity in an outdoor tank originally built by the California Department of Fish and Wildlife to hold rescued seabirds and marine mammals following an oil spill. Strobel is conducting a series of behavioral tests designed to reveal the effectiveness of each of Selka's senses.

I visited just days after Strobel and Selka had been introduced, so they were just getting to know each other. Selka was exploring her new environment, a twenty-foot-diameter tank filled four feet deep with seawater pumped from the ocean a quarter mile away. Hanging from a walkway across the tank was a mass of artificial kelp that researchers refer to as "car wash kelp," the same material that hangs from the ceiling at automatic car-wash centers and is slowly dragged across your car to scrub the dirt from your vehicle. As I watched, Strobel poured a bucket of ice into a small kiddie pool at the edge of the tank, which prompted Selka to jump out of the water. It was feeding time. Hidden amid the ice were shrimp and large pieces of clam meat, part of the otter's training in how to find food.

Propped on the edge of the pink pool not five feet from where I stood, Selka was a stunning beauty. Her lustrous mahogany coat shone from every angle, reminding me of my grandmother's mink stole. Not a hair was out of place—even her whiskers appeared well coiffed—unlike some wild otters that often look more like Albert Einstein than Jennifer Aniston. And she almost seemed to pose to make sure I noticed her stylishness.

Despite the abundant food before her, Selka didn't appear to be in any rush to dig in. She knew she had no competition for the delicacies concealed beneath the ice, so she deliberately pawed through the cubes, selected the item she desired, and carefully placed it in her mouth before proceeding to the next one. Once, she even yawned between bites, briefly showing off her incisors, which appeared unnecessarily large for the requirements of the meal. The longer she took to eat, however, the longer she was out of the water and baking in the hot sun, where she could quickly become over-heated. She seemed to sense the approaching discomfort, so she slowly slid over the edge of the shallow kiddie pool and sprawled on her belly in the ice while continuing to search for the rest of her hidden meal. As she luxuriated in the refreshing tub, forcing her head and shoulders beneath the ice cubes—and once even rolling over to do a quick backstroke—I could almost sense her feeling of relief.

Soon enough, Selka had found and consumed every bit of her food and leapt back into her large blue tank. She was purposely not offered molllusks, since she hadn't yet learned how to open them. "Older otters are like a machine at finding food," said Tinker. "A two-year-old like Selka might take four or five minutes to open a crab, something an older otter could do in thirty seconds. It emphasizes their specialization skills," which Selka had not yet developed.

But what she did have were innate senses that required no training to develop. According to Strobel, the little that is known about otter senses primarily involves their vision. She said sea otter vision is a mixed bag. Based on their eye anatomy, they appear to see equally well in the air and in the water, and they are adapted for life in a shallow-water environment where they must function in both the bright light above the water and the reduced light below. Unlike the deep-diving marine mammals like elephant seals, which are well adapted to very dark conditions, sea otters do not see well in the dark. Strobel said that an eye adapted for seeing in the air is usually not going to see well underwater, and vice versa. "Humans are a great example of that," she said.

Sea otters have a flat or lenticular lens common to terrestrial mammals, enabling them to see well in the air, whereas most marine mammals have a spherical lens more adapted to life in the marine environment. But when otters dive beneath the surface, they are able to—with what scientists call an accommodative mechanism—force their lenses to bulge outward to create the spherical shape that allows them to see better underwater. "We don't really know how it works," Strobel said, "but we assume a muscle can change where the fluid is and create differences in pressure."

As for their hearing, it's not particularly good when compared to other marine mammals, although it's still better than humans' hearing. But sea otters don't seem to need excellent hearing. Their prey is all rather silent, and the ocean is quite noisy, so they do not appear to have developed any special adaptations to hear especially well. While humans can hear in the range of 20 hertz to 20 kilohertz, sea otters have a slightly wider hearing range in the air—5 hertz to 32 kilohertz—while underwater they lose much of the lower frequencies and can hear sounds only above 250 hertz. However, their hearing seems to be particularly tuned to the frequency range between 8 and 16 kilohertz, which may be the frequency of the calls of sea otter pups. Communication between mother and pup is believed to be the primary sound that they need to detect. Because mothers and pups regularly get separated, they vocalize to find each other—the pup repeatedly squeals to call for its mother, and the mother responds with a slightly lower sound until they are reunited. Whether they use their hearing in any significant way outside of this social context is uncertain.

Tim Tinker isn't convinced that sea otters don't have extraordinary hearing, though. He said they seem particularly skilled at detecting and interpreting the danger inherent in the sounds of the boat and equipment he uses to capture sea otters for his research. "They're pretty amazing at hearing us," he said. "Maybe it's more about detecting a particular signal. They seem to know the sound of our dive equipment being put into the water. But for everything else, their hearing isn't so great."

Almost nothing is known about the sea otter's sense of smell, although as Mustelids otters come from a history of animals that use scent in territory marking and mate finding. Like many mammals, they are known to smell each other when they first meet, especially around the nether regions. But no studies have yet been conducted to reveal more about their olfactory capabilities.

The same is true of their sense of taste, although they appear to have very strong food preferences in captivity. They love shrimp and they avoid squid, for instance, so it is clear that they can tell the difference between the two. But they also may be able to detect some degree of toxicity in clams and other invertebrate prey. One study suggests that sea otters can taste a little bit of a clam and determine whether it is infected with the toxic algae that causes paralytic shellfish poisoning, something that humans are unable to do. The researchers fed clams containing various levels of the toxin to captive sea otters, and they found the animals could detect the toxin and avoided the clams with the highest levels. Of the clams containing low levels of the toxin, the otters ate only the nontoxic parts, especially avoiding the highly toxic siphons. Juvenile otters were unable to make this distinction.

Tinker has observed a similar behavior in the wild sea otters he has studied. He said that otters prefer to eat sea urchins when they are gravid with eggs, and after tasting them they sometimes discard those that have already spawned. "I've seen them bring up an urchin, take one bite, and throw it away," he said. "They do that in March right after the urchins spawn. It's like a taste test. You see them taste it and then decide whether to discard it or accept it."

Perhaps sea otters' most important sense is their tactile abilities, defined primarily by the use of their forepaws and whiskers. Strobel described "the stereotypical sea otter behavior" as feeling around for everything they can get their hands on and manipulating it to learn about it. "They're always feeling new things, even if they're not even looking at it," she said. And their use of tools is another indication of the importance of their sense of touch. "They're very extractive predators. They pick prey that they are forced to handle and extract something [from]. Just from observations, it seems like an incredibly strong and important sense for them." A 1968 study of the brains of various otter species found that the portion of the brain dedicated to tactile stimuli is enlarged compared to that of other Mustelid species.

Less is known about the use of their whiskers, which relay tactile information to their brains. Although sea otters are more closely related to terrestrial otters, their whiskers are more similar to those of seals and sea lions. Sea otters have about 120 whiskers, which is about the same as most seals, and the internal anatomy of their whiskers is also more like that of seals and sea lions than other species of otters. Whisker hair follicles are made up of collagen capsules containing flexible tissues, blood-filled sinuses, and nerves. When whisker hairs move, they send information to the brain via axons in vibrissal nerves. The sensitivity of each hair follicle is determined by the number of axons in the vibrissal nerves. Like seals and sea lions, sea otters have about 1,340 axons, nearly three times as many as river otters do, suggesting that the whiskers are highly sensitive.

Tinker believes that sea otters use their whiskers in some way for foraging, though he isn't sure exactly how. He told me that some of the otters he has captured in soft sediment areas of Alaska, like Zachar Bay and Clam Lagoon in the Aleutians, have whiskers that are worn down to stubble on one side of their face. "That's something we'd never seen anywhere else," he said. "You travel two kilometers away to the outer coast where they're eating urchins, and they all had normal-size whiskers. That tells us that they're using their whiskers for something in that soft-sediment area.

We don't know what, though, because we've never been under the water with them." He speculated that the stubble is a by-product of their sliding one side of their face against abrasive material as they search and dig for clams. But why just one side? "I've seen pictures of them swimming along with one side of their face down," he said. "They could be detecting something on the bottom that way. They could be looking for a siphon hole from a clam or detecting the flow of water coming from a siphon. Those are clues that maybe a whisker could help them with."

But, he admits, no one really knows.

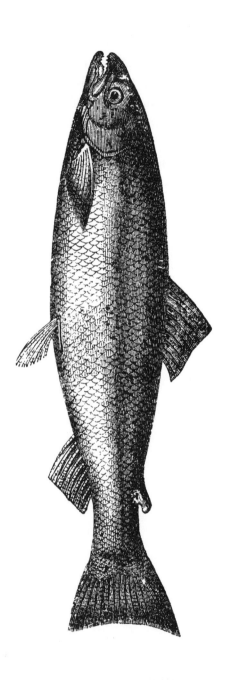

Chapter 5: Surrogate Mothers

IN THE OFFICE of the Sea Otter Research and Conservation program on the roof of the Monterey Bay Aquarium, Karl Mayer stared at a computer screen showing images of four of the six tanks where rehabilitating sea otters could be observed remotely. One circular tank contained four male otters, two of which were destined for release back into the wild within days and two of which would remain permanently in captivity at a research facility in Santa Cruz. Another tank contained a five-week-old female, while an eleven-day-old female received round-the-clock care in a third tank designated the intensive care unit. In the fourth tank, an adult female named Gidget, a permanent resident of the aquarium, cuddled on a platform in the middle of the tank with a young male who, just two days earlier, was introduced to Gidget as her surrogate pup. All of the young otters had been rescued after being found stranded on beaches on the central California coast.

As we watched, Mayer donned a black cape and dark welder's mask—an outfit the otter rehabilitators call the "Darth Vader look"—to bottle-feed the youngest of his charges, dubbed Otter 679. One of the most important strategies in raising a sea otter pup for release is to ensure it does not become imprinted on humans, hence the Darth Vader getup, which disguises Mayer so the otter doesn't know it is being cared for by a human. The feeding lasted just a couple minutes before Mayer placed the fluffy pup in the water to defecate, then dried her off and placed her on a platform beside the water. Mayer said this pup, discovered at Jalama Beach, which is near the southern end of the California sea otter's range, was probably born premature, and despite being nearly two weeks old, she was acting more like a one- or two-day-old otter. "She's circling the drain," he said, suggesting that her survival was far from certain. Every four hours an aquarium staff member or volunteer fed and groomed her, placed her in the water for thirty to forty minutes to acclimate her to her future environment, and then allowed her to nap.

Mayer returned to the office momentarily to make some notes before quickly turning around to visit the other young female otter, which was being introduced to solid food for the first time. Captive sea otter pups are fed only formula until they are about four weeks old. For the next four weeks they get a combination of formula and solid food, before being weaned from the formula at eight weeks of age. Pups begin to shed their fluffy natal pelage when they are a month old—a process that lasts four or five weeks—after which they no longer float like a cork and can begin to learn to dive beneath the surface of the water.

Mayer described his job as "a nonstop care scenario" in which he is continually assessing which otter needs what and when, and directing a team of four staff members and sixty-five students and volunteers to administer whatever care is necessary. Throughout our conversation, we were frequently interrupted by volunteers with questions and minor emergencies that Mayer had to address. He is in charge of everything at the aquarium that has to do with stranded sea otters, from responding to calls about injured otters and caring for them for sometimes months at a time, to determining animal-care protocols, training and supervising staff and volunteers, and coordinating the release of the animals and their postrelease tracking. It isn't at all what he initially envisioned for a career. Mayer thought he was going to become an attorney. But after volunteering at a marine-mammal rehabilitation center and spending a semester studying marine science at Woods Hole Oceanographic Institution, he decided to pursue a career in fisheries. After a stint as a fisheries observer for the National Marine Fisheries Service, he landed a part-time position in 1993 at the Monterey Bay Aquarium rehabilitating sea otters. He turned what he thought was going to be a brief stop into a lifelong career, and as the aquarium's otter activities grew and evolved, his role grew right along with them.

It's a rare day that the sea otter rehabilitation team at the aquarium does not get a phone call about a stranded sea otter. The six tanks available for rehabilitating otters at the aquarium are almost always occupied. One of Mayer's greatest struggles is creating space to accommodate additional stranded otter pups. But because there are few other licensed otter-rehabilitation facilities in California, the aquarium is the first responder.

The Marine Mammal Stranding Network in California, a group of non-profit organizations, biologists, and volunteers who respond to animals found stranded or injured on local beaches, has been in operation since 1975. Managed primarily by the National Marine Fisheries Service, it responds to six to eight hundred calls each year about stranded seals, sea lions, dolphins, sea otters, and other animals along the six hundred miles of the state's central and northern coastline. When environmental officials, beach or park attendants, or anyone else observes a stranded marine mammal, they call the center, and if the animal is a sea otter, that call is directed to Mayer's office.

Few stranded adult sea otters are captured and treated unless their injury is human caused, like a boat strike, fishing gear entanglement, or gunshot. In most cases, stranded adults are typically too far gone by the time they make it up on a beach and are discovered. Due to their high metabolism, if they haven't eaten in a day or more, their system begins to shut down. Stranded adults are usually diseased or geriatric and untreatable, and euthanasia is often the most humane option. That is especially true if the animal is an adult male, which biologists say have little value to the overall population. Rehabilitating and releasing adult males in an area that is already at carrying capacity could do more harm than good by displacing other wild sea otters. "We really can't justify rehabilitating adult males," Mayer said. "Adult females are really the most important component of the population because they're the reproducers."

That's not to say, however, that stranded adult male sea otters— or any others—will be left on the beach to fend for themselves. If there are people and dogs around and the otter is not exhibiting a flight response, the stranding team will intercede to protect it. Mayer said that those are often immature animals, in what he calls "the young and dumb category," that don't know they should avoid people and other large animals. In that case, the team may simply capture and relocate the otter.

If it's a pup, the approach is entirely different. The first step in assessing a stranded otter pup is to see if it can be reunited with its mother in the wild. Sometimes the two are separated inadvertently and just can't find each other. In about 10 percent of pup-stranding cases, the response team is successful at reuniting mothers and pups. If that doesn't work, or if the pup appears unhealthy or malnourished, it is captured and brought to the aquarium.

Regardless of the animal's age, once it arrives at the aquarium, it is thoroughly examined by veterinarian Mike Murray to identify any physiological reasons for why it stranded and to determine how to address any medical issues. Then comes the surprisingly challenging process of feeding the otter. "Here's an animal that has probably been struggling to eat and is obviously going to be hungry, so it should be a slam dunk to get it to eat, but it doesn't really work that way," Mayer said. That is often the case with recently weaned pups that have stranded due to an intestinal parasite they get from eating sand crabs. If the otter finds itself in sandy habitat, sand crabs can be abundant and easy for it to catch and consume. But the crab parasite eventually perforates the otter's intestinal wall, causing considerable pain and an unwillingness to eat.

Young pups require round-the-clock care during their first weeks at the aquarium, but by the eighth week they are ready to be introduced to a surrogate mother who will teach them how to feed themselves and survive in the wild. But that's a relatively recent development in the otter-rehabilitation program.

THE MONTEREY BAY AQUARIUM opened to the public in 1984, and sea otters played an important role from the very beginning, in part because of the facility's location in the center of the otters' California range. The aquarium's very first veterinarian, Tom Williams, had a personal interest in the species and even raised some sea otter pups in his bathtub at home before the rehabilitation program got under way. He conducted some basic research on sea otters in those early days, and when the aquarium began receiving calls about stranded otters—

some even before it opened—an exhibit originally designed to house seabirds was converted for sea otters. It has been one of the aquarium's most popular exhibits ever since.

Little was known about how best to care for captive sea otters when the exhibit first opened, and even less was known about how to rear them so they could be released back into the wild. Stranded pups were initially raised by a group of volunteers who treated them as if they were their own children. Karl Mayer described it as a hands-on, intensive, round-the-clock process during which the pups bonded with their caregivers so much that the animals couldn't be left alone. Early attempts to release them back into the wild were met with little success. The first male on permanent exhibit, Roscoe, was a recaptured animal. Little effort was made to monitor released otters back then, so little is known about how well they fared, though some—like Roscoe—were so habituated to people that they created problems by climbing on marina docks and interacting with scuba divers, kayakers, and fishermen.

There were also concerns that the captive-reared pups weren't learning how to survive on their own in the wild, so an ocean-swimming program was developed to introduce them to the marine environment and how to find food. Every day Mayer and his colleagues donned wet suits and took the pups into the bay just beyond the aquarium, taking advantage of the fact that the otters had bonded with humans and would not swim away. Every time Mayer would dive to the seafloor to look for otter prey, the pups followed alongside and learned how to do it themselves. Eventually Mayer found himself swimming with sea otter pups for several hours every day, a job that sounds to me like the ideal occupation.

"I learned an incredible amount about sea otters and sea otter behavior from going through that process," Mayer said.

"Obviously it's a pretty intimate sea otter–eye view of their life, learning what it takes to hold your breath and go down to the bottom and find prey items and bring them back up and crack them. The pups are really tethered to you. The first couple times you go out there you're scared you're going to lose them, and then you quickly realize there's no way you're going to lose them. They're glued to you."

While the swimming program appeared to help the otters survive in the wild, they were still bonded to their human caregivers. And as the aquarium began to ramp up its efforts to monitor the otters after release, they repeatedly found that they had to intercede in human-otter conflicts by recapturing the animals and relocating them elsewhere. So in 1999 Mayer decided to use a disguise during the hand-rearing process while also continuing to swim with them in the ocean. It wasn't enough. The otter pups continued to create conflicts with people once they were released.

Everything changed, however, when an adult female sea otter arrived at the aquarium in 2001. Given the name Toola, she was found to have toxoplasmosis, a disease caused by a parasite found in infected prey and resulting in a neurological disorder that manifests in grand mal seizures. While the aquarium treated her for several months, it was discovered that she was pregnant, and she eventually gave birth to a stillborn pup, which is a common symptom of toxoplasmosis. In what Mayer described as "extraordinarily fortuitous circumstances," a two-week-old male pup was discovered stranded on Del Monte Beach in Monterey just twelve hours after Toola gave birth. Although aquarium officials had discussed the possibility of eventually attempting to raise stranded pups with a surrogate mother, and they had even tried it once, they could not have arranged it any better. Toola was ready to care for a pup, and the pup was in need of a mother to take care of him. So Toola's stillborn pup was pulled away from her and replaced with the stranded pup—called Otter 217—and the two immediately began nursing. "We essentially had the prototype surrogacy unfold before our eyes," Mayer said.

This unplanned experiment spawned what has become a tremendously successful and scientifically proven method of raising young pups in captivity and releasing them into the wild. "The most important thing we realized about the developmental process is the bond with mom. The environment they're reared in is less important," Mayer said. "Even though it's a very difficult transition they have to make into an unfamiliar ocean environment, they instinctually will make that transition. But the biggest factor for their success is eliminating the human habituation. That wound up being the biggest detriment to the survival of the pups."

Pups are usually introduced to their surrogate mother at about eight weeks of age, and they remain together for four or five months before weaning. The first step is to remove the surrogate from the public exhibit several days before being introduced to the pup. The surrogacy process is somewhat stressful and energy demanding for the mother, so she is given extra attention throughout. She is placed into the surrogacy tank about twenty-four hours before the pup arrives to give her time to acclimate. "When the females come off the exhibit, it's a little bit of a negative for them," Mayer said. "The exhibit is kind of their happy place, and behind the scenes oftentimes isn't as much. We don't want the pup going in when she might be more likely to interpret the pup as being associated with that negative change, so there has to be a gap time." When the pup is first dropped into the tank with the surrogate, they are watched closely to see what happens. Sometimes they bond immediately; more often it takes a little time. The caretakers can sometimes use food to get the two animals to interact with each other. Some precocious pups have been known to dive and feed independently and the surrogate ends up being nothing more than a companion animal.

Mayer said that the more typical situation is that the pup initially becomes very focused on the female, following her around and nudging her, which causes the surrogate to try to avoid the pup. After a few hours of that, they may be separated before trying again the next day. And the next. Eventually they form a bond, but there is considerable variability from pup to pup and from surrogate to surrogate. Rosa, who had just completed the surrogacy of her twelfth pup when I visited, is very predictable. She apparently knows what is expected of her, and she bonds quickly with each new pup. The other current surrogates are new to the process, so their maternal behaviors vary. Abby, who was with her third pup at the time of my visit, was not sharing food with her pup, although she had with the previous one. And sometimes things change within one surrogacy, as when Abby started out with little interest in a pup, then became very maternal, and later lost interest again, as if she wanted the process to be over.

Regardless of the variations in the process, the surrogacy program has been tremendously successful. More than thirty pups have been raised by nine surrogate mothers and released into the wild, and about 70 percent of those released have survived the first year, which is about equivalent to the pup survival rate in the wild population and well above the 10 to 15 percent success rate using the prior hand-rearing method.

Otter pups are released about four to eight weeks after being weaned and two to four weeks after having a transmitter implanted and flipper tag attached. During those last few weeks before release, the animals are kept in a tank with several other otters to learn how to interact in a setting more analogous to their life in the wild. But the release process can be complicated. It doesn't always work the first time. They sometimes can't find food and quickly lose energy, or they wander into a marsh or other habitat in which they are unlikely to survive, or they run into predators or other difficulties. They have only a three- or four-day window of time to figure out all those things before their body starts to shut down. So before they're too far gone, the animal may be recaptured and rehabilitated for a few weeks before being released again, when the success rate climbs from 40 to 70 percent. Those few that still struggle and need to be recaptured again are nearly always successful on the third release.

"Part of the goal of our surrogacy studies has been to really define success by as rigorous a criteria as we could," Mayer said. "With our guys, we've followed some of the surrogate-reared animals for more than eleven years, so we've got a long-term data set with an increasing sample size." That tracking has found that the surrogate-raised female pups have gone on to give birth to more than twenty-five pups of their own, and the survival rate of those pups matches that of the rest of the wild population. It's a success story of which Mayer and all those involved are rightfully proud.

THE MONTEREY BAY AQUARIUM has been a major player in sea otter research for many years. Its veterinarian, Mike Murray, has surgically implanted transmitters in nearly every sea otter that is part of any research project in California. And biologist Michelle Staedler and her crew of volunteers and interns handle the daily tracking of those animals year in and year out. Graduate students from several universities regularly get access to the captive and stranded otters for any number of research projects, and Murray and the aquarium staff conduct veterinary and husbandry studies to better understand sea otter health and how best to care for them. It's an expensive undertaking, partly because of the large quantity of food each captive otter must eat.

But Andy Johnson, who leads the aquarium's Sea Otter Research and Conservation program, is always pushing to do more. He has been working with sea otters for more than thirty years, starting at SeaWorld in San Diego and later at the Vancouver Aquarium before landing in Monterey in 1998. While he's proud of the important role the aquarium plays, he notes that much of what it accomplishes is done with an informal alliance he helped establish to study and conserve sea otters in California; it includes scientists at UC Santa Cruz, UC Davis, the US Fish and Wildlife Service, the US Geological Survey, and the California Department of Fish and Wildlife. Johnson describes the alliance as an interdependent group that works together to achieve whatever needs to be accomplished. The alliance relies on Tim Tinker to synthesize existing research to determine what questions need to be answered next, and it pools its resources to get it done.

Johnson said that the aquarium doesn't ignore the policy arena, either. All the research in the world won't protect sea otters if regulators and government officials make decisions that place the animals in harm's way. The aquarium works with Friends of the Sea Otter, Defenders of Wildlife, and whoever else it can recruit to help pass legislation to benefit otters. These groups worked together, for instance, to establish the California Sea Otter Fund, a mechanism on California state income tax forms that enables the public to donate to support sea otter research and conservation. Since 2007 it has provided about $300,000 each year for competitive research grants and state conservation efforts, including a pathology program that determines the cause of death of otters that wash ashore. A bill to reauthorize the fund for another five years was passed by the California legislature in 2015.

My first visit to the Monterey Bay Aquarium occurred during Sea Otter Awareness Week in mid-September, when it was clear to everyone in attendance that sea otters are aquarium superstars. Hundreds of visitors lined up well before the aquarium opened, and as they filed inside they quickly came face to face with three sea otters housed in a two-story tank. Crowds of people standing six or seven deep around ten windows watched as Gidget, Ivy, and Kit went about their daily activities—diving, grooming, and rolling around. When the formal feeding program began, the adult humans watching were just as excited as the children. Cooing and giggling and more cooing were the typical reactions from observers of all ages and genders. I couldn't keep track of how many times I heard the visitors say the word "cute," but it was a lot.

The sea otter aquarists, as the staff are called, dragged large quantities of ice cubes to the edge of the exhibit, causing the otters to go into a playful frenzy, racing around the pool and leaping atop each other in what appeared to be a childlike effort to be first in line for a treat. As I watched from a behind-the-scenes observation platform, the ice was unceremoniously dumped into the water, and the animals thrashed about gathering as much of it as they could. One otter carried several ice chunks on her belly while holding one cube in each hand and chewing on another. A different otter protected a cube from thievery by stashing it in a pouch in her armpit, then dived to the bottom of the pool with her mouth full to quietly enjoy her booty. Their unbounded excitement, like a child's first moments at an amusement park, was contagious among those of us watching, causing the noise level in the building to rise markedly.

Soon the animals tired of the ice and looked like they were expecting something more. They gathered at the edge of the tank as the aquarists walked out on a rocky platform and fed them fish and clams by tossing the food onto the otters' bellies. Feeding-time behavior was the polar opposite of their previous behavior. The otters seemed entirely focused on filling their stomachs. While ice was a plaything, food was a meal. Instead of racing around and splashing, they calmly placed each morsel in their mouth, chewed and swallowed, and then waited for delivery of the next one. They paid no attention to the hordes of noisy visitors pounding on the glass tank, focusing instead on not dropping any crumbs—and when they inevitably did, they quickly dived to the bottom to retrieve them before surfacing for the rest of their meal.

Later, several plastic objects were tossed into the water, including a blue barrel that they aggressively clambered into and out of in what appeared to be a race through an obstacle course. The items were clearly intended as playthings, and the otters knew it. They chased and slapped each other, played a combination of keep-away and king of the hill, and scuffled and tussled until they were exhausted. Their high energy and nonstop activity made me exhausted, too.

So I wandered around the aquarium to a number of exhibits about sea otter research and physiology, then entered an auditorium to watch a short film about a rescued otter named Luna, whose first appearance on screen received a chorus of oohs and aahs from the audience. Before the video started, the man who introduced the program declared, "It's a scientific fact that sea otters are cute." No one in the audience disagreed.

BACK ON THE ROOF of the aquarium, Mayer gathered three helpers to move four juvenile otters from one tank to another so the
first tank could be cleaned. Despite the large size of the outdoor
tanks, they hold just two feet of water because the roof of the aquarium cannot support any more weight than that. Once the otters
had been relocated, it was time to groom the youngest otter again.
According to Mayer, pup grooming requires multiple steps. Large
towels are used to dry the outer guard hairs, while smaller towels
are used to groom the fine, dense inner fur. Flea combs and hair-
brushes are used next to fluff up the fur, and finger grooming mas-
sages the fur into layers and helps to remove mats in the fur. "The
process stimulates them to do it on their own," he said. "Eventually
they will instinctively do it themselves." But because humans are
not as efficient groomers as wild otters, captive otter pups tend to
have more bad hair days than wild ones do. "Wild moms are much
more proficient at it than we are," Mayer added.

Ever since I first learned that otter pups must be taught by their
mothers to groom themselves and that rescued otters are taught
by human surrogates, I have imagined that the job of baby otter
groomer at the aquarium may be the most desirable occupation on
earth. While I was not allowed to groom Otter 679 myself, I did get
to wear the Darth Vader gear and stand beside Mayer as he did the
deed. And it was just as adorable and heartbreaking as I envisioned.
Mayer lifted the tiny pup from the water and carried her like a
football to a platform beside the intensive care unit tank, where he
placed the otter on her back on a towel and fed her a dose of med-
icine from a syringe. She sat quietly looking like a child's stuffed
animal until Mayer inserted a needle beneath her skin to deliver

a large quantity of supplemental formula, which caused the infant otter to cry in loud, high-pitched wails. But as soon as he removed the needle, Otter 679—who would be transferred to SeaWorld in San Diego a month later and renamed Pumpkin—stopped crying and appeared to relax completely. Mayer took the edges of the towel the otter lay on and began a gentle process of rubbing the animal in short strokes from her head to her belly to her barely noticeable tail. He rolled her over to continue the process on her back, then finished the first round with a brief foot massage. Then he took a hairbrush to carefully work out the small matted spots in her fur, which caused her to squirm a bit. When Mayer placed the brush beside her to grab another towel, the animal leaned over and rubbed her chin on the brush herself. Despite her squirming, the brushing was obviously something she enjoyed. Another round of rubbing with the towel led Otter 679 to nudge Mayer's hand with her nose before lying back again to relax. She occasionally emitted a soft squeal like a whiny two-year-old child, as if the rubbing was uncomfortable, but the bleating became almost unbearable when Mayer set her in the water to float for a few minutes. At that moment, there was nothing I wanted more than to ease her discomfort. Instead, Mayer did so by removing Otter 679 from the water and giving her one more rub-down with the towel. Then it was time for more brushing, including on a spot behind her head that quieted her down completely. After turning on an overhead air dryer, Mayer finished by brushing the pup one more time. She shook her head once, then curled up and promptly fell asleep. The experience was the most precious fifteen minutes of my year.

Chapter 6: Stranded

THREE THOUSAND miles northwest of Monterey lies the city of Homer, Alaska, which is somewhat of an anomaly in the state. Long called the halibut-fishing capital of the world and, more recently, the "cosmic hamlet by the sea," the community of five thousand people lies at the very end of the road in south-central Alaska on the shores of Kachemak Bay; it is the southernmost town in the Alaska highway system. It's a community filled with a mix of fishermen and artists and those who depend on tourists for their living, with many divergent viewpoints among them, so its residents may be among the most liberal in a rather conservative state.

Homer's most distinguishing feature is the Homer Spit, a four-and-a-half-mile-long geological feature extending into Kachemak Bay that was recently called one of the one hundred best beaches in the United States. And while it's crammed full of restaurants, tourist shops, and marinas, it's also an ideal place to watch for seabirds, shorebirds, and marine mammals in the bay and along the shoreline. The tides are huge in Homer, with a gain of more than twenty feet at high tide, and low tides leave mudflats extending a quarter mile and more out from the wrack line. It's a great place to look for sea otters.

On our first drive out on the spit, Renay and I had several distant views of otters that were mostly loafing on their backs. On our next trip, we walked around the southernmost point, called Land's End, and while we had an excellent view of a Steller sea lion, there was an unexpected absence of otters. Unexpected because Homer has one of the highest densities of sea otters in the world. As a result, it's also the place in Alaska where the largest numbers of otters wash ashore dead, dying, or separated from their mothers.

We were in Homer in late May to meet Marc Webber, the deputy manager of the Alaska Maritime National Wildlife Refuge and one of the lead volunteers for the Alaska Marine Mammal Stranding Network. Like its counterpart in California, it responds to reports of stranded seals, sea lions, sea otters, and occasionally other species found on the entire coast of Alaska. Most of the reports are of otters, and most come from the Homer area because of its high number of beach walkers and its community-wide concern for the well-being of wildlife. Webber said the stranding network is mostly a waiting game for the volunteers, who wait for members of the public to call about a stranded animal, although in summer an intern routinely visits the beaches and the spit to look for otters. When we visited, Webber led us back out to the spit in search of stranded otters. A brief scan with our binoculars at several of the usual places revealed no dead otters, but we did see a few live ones, though not nearly as many as I had anticipated.

We ended up at Land's End again on a sixty-degree, sunny afternoon to watch for whatever wildlife we could find. Black-legged kittiwakes actively dived and swooped around a rip current where bait fish or some other edibles must have been just below the surface, and occasionally a few ducks—mostly white-winged scoters—and cormorants flew by. It wasn't long before otters began to appear. The first one was too far out to see well, and it disappeared shortly as it drifted with the current. A second otter gave us a much better look at itself. Its head was distinctively pale down to its shoulders, suggesting that it was an older animal. The otter repeatedly switched from swimming on its belly to porpoising briefly underwater, then rolling onto its back for a momentary bit of grooming, then whirling back to its belly again. And when it dived, it appeared to jump straight upward—much higher than I expected—before U-turning into a vertical dive, like my early days of doing a jackknife off the diving board at home. It was highly entertaining to watch.

Two more otters appeared briefly, well beyond the kittiwakes, but after we momentarily turned our heads away, we couldn't relocate them again. The next otter was fighting the current, but doing so with aplomb and little energy. Its head appeared gray brown, definitely not the blond of the first otter, and it spent most of its time on its back, leisurely kicking with its flippers to propel itself through the opposing current, as if it were no effort whatsoever. When the animal stopped, it raised its head up high, as if to get a better view above the waves—a behavior Tim Tinker calls periscoping—before sliding back beneath the surface. And then it returned to its back for a bout of grooming, starting with a lengthy scratching of its belly and chest, then rinsing its paws in the water and working on its face—first its cheeks and then its eyes and neck—before jackknifing below the surface.

At one point, we watched as a small powerboat approached an otter, veering slightly in the animal's direction, apparently to get a better look. A young girl sat on the bow staring straight at the animal, which didn't appear to change its behavior, nor did it get out of the way. Nothing deleterious happened, but Webber said that it was probably a violation of the Marine Mammal Protection Act. It's illegal to approach within one hundred yards of a marine mammal, he said. We also saw another boat zoom right by a different otter, seemingly oblivious to the animal's presence and not likely an intentional act. Again, the otter didn't move, as if the boater's behavior was a common occurrence and the animal was unbothered. But the action was illegal nonetheless.

IT TOOK A surprisingly long time for sea otters to recolonize the Homer area after the fur trade wiped them out. A small remnant population of otters just 180 miles away in the waters off the north end of Kodiak Island and another group in western Prince William Sound, even closer, survived the trade. But although a few individual otters were occasionally seen in Kachemak Bay in the 1960s—most presumed to be old males—it wasn't until the 1970s that observations increased in frequency and a permanent population was established. An aerial survey in 1975 found just eleven sea otters, and several monthly surveys the following year turned up as many as forty-nine animals, mostly across the bay in Seldovia. Based on those surveys, it was estimated that the region had about four hundred sea otters, though most were believed to be males from the recolonized population on the outer Kenai Peninsula, which had been established from western Prince William Sound otters seeking new territories. Sea otters were not surveyed again in the area for twenty years. In 1994, 151 were counted by boat, including mothers with pups, and 355 were observed from the air, leading researchers to estimate a population of 1,104. A 2002 survey believed to be the most accurate to that date concluded that 912 sea otters lived in Kachemak Bay, but just six years later the population had more than tripled to 3,724, and by 2012 it had grown to nearly 6,000.

"That total is well within the carrying capacity of this area, but those are big jumps in population over relatively short periods, and we're not entirely sure why," said Angela Doroff, an otter biologist and research coordinator at the Kachemak Bay National Estuarine Research Reserve. Over breakfast in Homer, she told me that the most recent jump could have happened from natural reproduction alone, but she believes that the previous population jump from 912 to 3,724 was likely due to a major influx of male otters from elsewhere into the area. As a result, she said, the Kachemak Bay population of sea otters has many more males than females, and that causes a great deal of stress on the female population.

"Once an adult female weans her pup, she's in really poor condition," Doroff said. "It takes a lot of energy to feed themselves and a growing pup, so they're depleted, they're bony. By the time that pup is ready to wean, they've used everything they've got, and they're more subject to disease. They also get mating injuries from rogue males who are really aggressive. They get torn up, and they get infections, and they die. So we're losing the reproductive component of the population. And I think it's probably because we have a large group of males that has upset the balance."

The skewed sex ratio also leads to more frequent pup-stealing, a food-stealing technique that occurs when a male sea otter holds a pup hostage until its mother gives up its prey. Doroff told me the story of watching a female otter trying to dive for food without allowing nearby males to harass her pup. On one brief foraging dive, the mother otter returned to the surface to find three males tugging at her pup. At length, she fought off the males and rescued her pup, and she even succeeded in retaining a clam hidden in her armpit. But more often than not a mother's prey is sacrificed to protect her young.

The sea otter population in the Homer area is also unusual in that its habitat is quite different from that used by sea otters nearly everywhere else in its range. Instead of hard-bottomed habitat with abundant kelp, Kachemak Bay has mostly soft sediments free of kelp. And since the otters aren't restricted to areas of kelp, they are free to roam and feed wherever food can be found. That means sea otters are often found feeding miles from shore. In fact, in the 1970s and '80s, rafts of about one hundred sea otters were regularly reported to be seen thirty miles offshore in areas where soft sediments extended far out on the broad continental shelf, according to Doroff, and the animals almost never came to shore because they didn't have to. Everything they needed to eat and raise their young could be found offshore. The soft sediments and absence of kelp in Kachemak Bay also means that the diet of sea otters there is much different from that of otters elsewhere. Instead of eating urchins, crabs, and sea cucumbers for the bulk of their diet, sea otters in the Homer area eat primarily clams and mussels, with only an occasional crab, urchin, or snail.

One thing about sea otters that has intrigued Doroff for many years is their remarkable ability to find food where none is apparent to human eyes. A member of the International Union for Conservation of Nature's otter specialist group, she has studied the foraging habits of sea otters throughout their range. She says it is unusually difficult to study otter feeding behaviors in Homer because the animals often feed so far offshore that it is challenging to observe them. But in Prince William Sound after the Exxon Valdez oil spill, she conducted extensive studies of their foraging practices, watching to see what food item they captured every time they dived below the surface. She found that the animals were successful on 97 percent of their foraging dives, each of which lasted about ninety seconds, and most of the time they returned to the surface with more than one clam. But when she put on a wet suit and scuba gear to observe the habitat and availability of prey for herself, she swam around for forty-five minutes and only found one clam. "I had visions of what it was going to look like down there, but I was all wrong," she said. "I don't know what they're cuing on, but I didn't have it. They have a very different set of tools than we do."

That impressive ability to find prey on or beneath the seafloor, along with their voracious appetite, has caused some in Homer to long for the days when sea otters were extirpated from the area and shellfish were more abundant. Local residents enjoyed the days of unregulated clamming in the 1960s and '70s when it was easy to fill a fifty-five-gallon drum with several varieties of clams in half a day. Those were also the days when king and Dungeness crab, shrimp, and herring were abundant and commercial fisheries for those species thrived. While sea otters have had a role in the depletion of crab and clam numbers, they are often blamed for the overfishing of species they don't feed on.

"Some people feel a great sadness because they remember a much more bountiful time—bountiful in a consumptive sense," Doroff said. "They feel like things are out of balance, that it's wrong, that there should be predator control because otters are wrecking the ecosystem." But, she pointed out, sea otters evolved with all of those species and never exterminated them through hundreds of millennia. It wasn't until the fur trade wiped out the otters that a shift took place in the ecosystem. And it was a shift that people liked and one from which they made a living. Now that the system is shifting back to normal, a small segment of the human population is fighting to restore the previous status quo. But so far it has been a losing battle.

"Sea otters are certainly a key player, there's no doubt about it, but so are humans," said Doroff. "What I think we fail to realize is that there are more feet on the planet trying to extract more and more resources. The multiplier effect is huge. There is a whole human pressure on the system that has never been there before, and it's something that we don't acknowledge readily."

Although the commercial harvest of most marine invertebrates in Kachemak Bay is unlikely to ever return to its former levels, regardless of whether sea otters remain, there are emerging shellfisheries that may achieve commercial success alongside a thriving otter population. In a few small bays on the south shore of Kachemak Bay, several entrepreneurs have established oyster aquaculture operations, and while a few otters have found ways to access the lantern nets holding the oysters, the animals have not been a significant problem to the farmers. The practice offers a bit of hope for the next generation of fishermen in Homer.

RENAY AND I FOUND no stranded otters during the two days we were in Homer, though five were reported the previous week. So we left Homer and drove about two hours to Seward, where three giant cruise ships were anchored and the tiny tourist village was filled with vacationers wandering around looking for souvenirs and a fresh seafood lunch. We pulled into the Alaska SeaLife Center at the southern end of town, where we met Brett Long, the husbandry director responsible for all animal care at the facility. He works with a team of veterinarians and a staff of forty-two that cares for every creature in the place, from huge Steller sea lions and harbor seals to puffins, crabs, and a giant octopus. Long described the center, which opened in 1998, as "a research facility with a public interface," even though it looks like what most people would call a modern aquarium. It was built in large part with funds provided by the settlement of the Exxon Valdez oil spill, and even though it doesn't have the necessary infrastructure to clean oiled animals in the likely event of a future oil spill—the facility doesn't have the equipment to separate the oil from the water after it is washed from the animals—the staff and equipment will probably still play a significant role.

Long said the center is charged with responding to any stranded marine mammal in south-central Alaska that is not on the US endangered species list, rehabilitating it, and releasing it back where it was found, if appropriate. The National Marine Fisheries Service can also ask staff of the center to help with animals stranded elsewhere in the state. They typically respond to thirty to fifty live animals per year, mostly harbor seals but also sea lions, fur seals, walruses, seabirds, and sea otters. It's an unexpectedly small number of rescued animals, considering the forty thousand miles of the Alaska coastline, especially when compared to the one thousand animals rescued each year in California along just three hundred miles of coastline. The difference, of course, is primarily due to the challenging geography and sparse human population in Alaska.

The facility rehabilitates about two sea otter pups each year, almost always from the Homer area, but has rehabilitated only two adult otters—what Long calls "little Tasmanian devils"—in the sixteen-year history of the center. Their limited experience with rehabilitating adult otters has been with those that can be quickly treated for minor injuries like a boat strike and released.

After a sea otter pup has been stabilized at the center for two to four weeks, it's time to determine its future home. Sea otters are in demand at aquariums around the world, but federal officials recently reinterpreted the rules for identifying appropriate sites to send them, making the process more complicated. Otters from the Aleutian Island and California populations are considered endangered, so it is illegal under the Marine Mammal Protection Act to export them outside of the United States. Those from south-central and Southeast Alaska, however, are not endangered and are therefore legal to export to aquariums abroad. Because most US aquariums that want sea otters already have as many as they can handle, they sometimes shuffle animals around to meet the legal requirements of where more recently stranded animals can go. For instance, if an otter pup from an endangered population strands, a US aquarium that has otters from nonendangered populations may send one of its otters back to the SeaLife Center so it can be sent abroad, and in return the aquarium will receive the otter from the endangered population. This otter shuffle provides legal and safe homes for all stranded sea otter pups. It's an expensive proposition, since the pups require constant care and grooming for several months before they can take care of themselves, but most aquariums seeking otters are willing to accept that cost and responsibility.

Not every aquarium abroad that wants a sea otter can have one, though. Aquariums first must have facilities that meet US animal-care standards, and they must have a government oversight system in place that will hold that facility to those standards. "They have to get their government to sign off on it, basically saying that if they don't hold the facility to our standards, we can come and take the animals back," Long explained. "A lot of foreign governments aren't willing to do that. And beyond Europe, the challenge is the philosophical approaches to animal care that are very different from what we require."

The governments of Denmark and France were the first to jump through the new legal hoops. When I visited the SeaLife Center, it was holding three sea otters destined for Danish and French aquariums that were completing their new exhibit spaces. Long escorted Renay and me behind the scenes of the center to see the future European residents. We walked through several double doors to a space that looked like a small laboratory and then into what could have been a tiny medium-security prison—beige walls and four gated sliding doors with small windows. I glanced through the first window to see a six-foot-square pool sunk four feet into the floor, with an area around it for lounging. It's a space typically used to rehabilitate seabirds and to hold sea otters for short periods. Quietly resting on their backs in the water were two six-month-old rescued otters named Agnes and Aurora, lying perpendicular to each other. They didn't remain quiet for long. As soon as she saw my face in the window, Agnes dived beneath the water and quickly emerged, squealing loudly, a grating noise that sounded like a high-pitched whistle or screaming little girls. It was not a normal sea otter vocalization but a learned behavior to get attention. Long said that baby otters scream all the time, but their mothers don't tolerate it for long. Their human caregivers, however, feel bad for the animals and let them get away with it or feed them to keep them quiet. Agnes just wanted to be fed and thought that our arrival signaled that it was feeding time. It wasn't, so she squealed repeatedly until long after we departed. Across the hall was a similar enclosure where Nuka, a four-year-old male sea otter in the midst of being shuffled from the Oregon Coast Aquarium to France, was perched on the edge of the pool waiting for mealtime. And a trip to Europe.

Chapter 7: Necropsy

THE MARINE MAMMALS Laboratory at the Alaska headquarters of the US Fish and Wildlife Service in Anchorage looks much like a lot of other scientific laboratories I've visited. But this one is designated primarily for conducting necropsies of marine mammals, especially sea otters. Its mix-and-match group of cabinets was filled with chemicals, tools, and various supplies and equipment for dissecting fresh or frozen carcasses. Large picnic coolers containing recently delivered animals or tissues lined one wall. A walk-in freezer was filled with twenty years' worth of animal parts—mostly sea otters, but also seals, sea lions, walruses, and polar bears—that had yet to be a priority in any scientific study. Two industrial saws sat waiting to be used to carve through bones and sinew. Tissue samples and skulls sat in jars, soaking in formalin. And inside a ventilated laboratory hood sat a plastic tub filled with dermestid beetles gnawing the flesh from animal bones.

The centerpiece of the room was a stainless-steel table about ten feet long with a sink at one end to allow a putrid array of animal fluids and chemicals to be easily washed away. Where those liquids go, I didn't know, and I really didn't want to find out. Lying on the table was a large black trash bag containing a male sea otter that had been thawing for four days. It was an animal identified as FW14026, meaning that it was the twenty-sixth sea otter to be necropsied in 2014 by the Fish and Wildlife Service. It had been found dead two weeks earlier on Holiday Island, a small island a half mile off the east-central coast of Kodiak Island, near the village of Kodiak. Since the sea otter was part of the Aleutian Island stock of otters that is listed on the US endangered species list, determining its cause of death was a priority.

Renay and I had been invited to observe the necropsy, which would be performed by Kristin Worman, a Fish and Wildlife Service biological technician who conducts several such procedures each week. After an extensive orientation session, she asked Renay to assist with the procedure, and Renay enthusiastically agreed. Together they weighed the bagged otter and determined it to be forty-nine pounds, which is on the light side and suggested that it may not have been eating well in the weeks leading to its death. When they opened the bag to remove the animal, the odor in the lab quickly went from a clean antiseptic smell to the stench of decomposition; either it dissipated quickly or I just got used to it, because I hardly noticed it a few minutes later. The otter's fur was soggy and matted as Worman began a general evaluation of the animal's physical condition, noting minor scarring on the nose, flippers, and paws.

After University of Alaska students Amy Kirkham and Quinsey Jorgensen joined us, the real work began. Kirkham used a pair of pliers to remove one of the otter's premolar teeth for later use in accurately determining the age of the animal; I later learned that Otter FW14026 was four years old. Then she pulled out a handful of the animal's whiskers for future analysis of stable isotopes that provide an indication of what the otter had been eating in recent weeks. At the same time, Worman used a scalpel to make an incision down the length of the otter from throat to tail. She and Renay had prepared a dozen scalpels in advance knowing that the animal's thick fur would rapidly dull the blades. As Jorgensen took notes and stored tissue samples, the rest of the group spent the next thirty minutes completely skinning the otter by pulling back on the fur and carefully cutting away the flesh. The pelt, which provides little information about cause of death, was unceremoniously dropped into the trash.

The furless otter looked gruesome, like a red and maroon E. T. with big teeth and a long rib cage, but I was the only one focused on the entire animal. The rest of the humans in the room were swarming around the table and digging into the carcass to collect very specific tissue samples for measurement and later study—testes, lymph nodes, thyroid, adrenal gland, even the tonsils, which can provide evidence of bacteria entering the body in its diet. Kirkham quickly decapitated the otter and worked for twenty minutes to remove the flesh from its head so she could cut open its skull to examine the brain and collect samples of the cerebrum and cerebellum. At the same time, Worman removed and weighed the major organs, each of which was closely examined for abnormalities. Any apparent blemish on the surface of an organ was sliced open to determine if the blemish extended deep into the tissue, which could be an indication of disease. Throughout the process, they called out numbers for Jorgensen to record on data forms, and when she was too busy, they wrote the numbers in otter blood on the steel table.

Worman then collected a urine sample in a syringe and noted that it appeared red and cloudy, a sign of bladder inflammation. The gallbladder was examined for signs of parasites—only one was found—and a sample of bile was collected to test for toxins from harmful algal blooms. Its liver was found to be unusually small with "sharp margins," another sign that the otter hadn't been eating well.

There was nothing in the colon or stomach, but the latter had signs of a bleeding ulcer. The lungs, which Worman said should be "pink and fluffy," had lost their form and appeared rubbery. She looked through yards and yards of intestines and found just one thorny-headed worm, a common parasite, then struggled to collect a sample of heart blood because most of the blood had already clotted. Next she measured the heart valves and followed the path of blood through the heart and lungs, looking for abnormalities. There was no smoking gun in all of these findings, just a litany of minor issues that indicated the otter was unhealthy.

Three and a half hours after beginning, during one of the last steps in the necropsy, Worman found what she believed killed the otter—a pea-size lesion in the aortic valve, where the blood exits the heart. Consisting of numerous colonies of bacteria, the lesion is the diagnostic sign of vegetative valvular endocarditis, which leads to congestive heart failure and a variety of infections. It's a common cause of death in otters in south-central Alaska.

VEGETATIVE VALVULAR endocarditis was the official cause of death of sea otter FW14026, but its heart condition was caused by one of several varieties of the streptococcus bacterium. Strep syndrome, as the otter biologists and pathologists call it, is the leading cause of death of sea otters in Alaska. A 10-year study of 144 dead sea otters found that 60 of the animals died as a direct result of strep. But what causes strep syndrome is entirely unknown. Verena Gill, a US Fish and Wildlife Service biologist who studied the health of Alaska's sea otter population for a dozen years before transferring to the Bureau of Ocean Energy Management in 2014, told me that the general consensus is that strep is probably caused by something stressing an otter's immune system and making it more susceptible to disease. "At first we thought maybe they were getting it from wounds or from bad teeth," she said. "But now we're starting to think it's normal for sea otters to carry these kind of organisms around, and it grows when their immune system is suppressed. What causes the stress could be anything—it could be another disease, we don't really know. But they come in and they die from a growth on their heart valve and then they test positive for strep. We have not gotten to the bottom of what's causing it."

The heart condition that results from strep syndrome was first discovered in sea otters in Kachemak Bay in Homer in 1998, and by 2006 there were so many dead otters washing up on beaches there that the government declared an "unusual mortality event," an official designation under the Marine Mammal Protection Act that requires immediate government action in response to a significant and unexpected die-off of a protected species. That's how Kristin Worman was hired by the Fish and Wildlife Service—first as a summer worker walking the beaches in Homer to collect sea otter carcasses for study and then in her current position conducting otter necropsies.

ONE OF THE SIGNIFICANT discoveries that came out of the work following the unusual mortality event declaration was an otter survey of Kachemak Bay that found thousands of sea otters in the area, when prior to that experts had believed the population totaled only about nine hundred animals. At first the biologists believed that the large number of dead sea otters was not unusual given that the otter population was much larger than originally thought. And even when so many of them were found to have died from strep syndrome, some biologists like Gill thought that strep was "just what they die of up here." But now she thinks otherwise. To have such a high proportion of sea otters die from this one disease was anything but natural, she said.

While strep syndrome remains the leading cause of death among otters in Alaska, they die from dozens of other things as well. Trauma, both human-caused and that administered by other animals, is second on the list. Typical mortality from trauma occurs due to boat strikes, gunshot wounds, injuries caused by fighting with other otters, mating trauma, and predation by killer whales. Bald eagles will occasionally capture and consume sea otter pups, as well. Legal hunting of sea otters by Native Alaskans is not included in studies of sea otter mortality, even though hunting may be the leading cause of death some years, with as many as 1,500 animals killed by hunters annually in recent years.

Most commonly, however, numerous factors contribute to the death of an otter. In the case of sea otter FW14026, when the test results came back on the various samples collected during its necropsy, it was found that in addition to strep syndrome it had a bacterium in its brain associated with meningitis. That kind of finding is quite common. Gill said that it is extremely difficult to categorize the cause of death of most sea otters because so many different factors contribute. She recalled two otters that were struck by boats off Kodiak Island, but when they were tested it was found that they were loaded with huge levels of the biotoxin that causes paralytic shellfish poisoning. The boaters reported that the otters had barely moved as the boat approached, which, as it turns out, is a common behavior among otters affected by the toxin. So were the otters killed by the boat strike or by paralytic shellfish poisoning? Many otters that are found to have been killed by predators were ill from any number of diseases. And the predators—usually great white sharks in California and killer whales in the Aleutian Islands—probably sensed they were an easy target. While the predators struck the final blow on those otters, the diseases were probably just as culpable for the death of those animals.

On the other hand, juvenile male sea otters will often die from what Gill says is stupidity. "One just packed his gut so much with mussels that he couldn't pass anything and died. Or they'll eat fish discards at the dock, because they're stupid and haven't figured out yet that's a bad idea, and they'll perforate their guts with fish bones. There are a lot of parasites in those fish discards, and the parasites will perforate their guts. One guy last week drowned, but he had eaten a lot of fish discards full of parasites, perforated his gut, and he drowned. But really the cause of death was stupidity."

Sea otters in Alaska have died from some rather strange things, too. Cancer is unexpectedly common, and otters die as a result of oil spills quite regularly, even in areas where an oil spill has not been reported. Phocine distemper, a virus that killed twenty thousand gray and harbor seals in Europe in 1988 and 2002, had never been recorded in the Pacific Ocean until it was found to be a contributing factor in the death of a number of sea otters in Alaska in the 2000s. Gill theorizes that it arrived via seals crossing the Northwest Passage. There has even been a case of a sea otter dying from histoplasmosis, an infection typically found in the Midwest that is caused by inhaling the spores of a fungus found in bird and bat droppings.

The good news from all of the health studies of sea otters in Alaska, especially the large number of carcasses turning up on the shores of Homer, is that there does not appear to be a disproportionate number of dead and dying otters in any particular age or gender group. "That's a hopeful sign," concluded Worman. "Since there isn't a specific segment of the population that is succumbing, it suggests that the population is generally healthy and thriving."

THE STORY OF sea otter health in California, however, is very different from that in Alaska. Strep syndrome, for instance, is hardly ever encountered in California, and when it is, pathologists look at it as a curiosity rather than a dire concern. According to Melissa Miller, a veterinary pathologist at the California Marine Wildlife Veterinary Care and Research Center in Santa Cruz, shark bites appear to be the leading cause of death among sea otters in California, but she is more concerned with the effects of disease-causing microorganisms and pollutants, especially those that originate on land. There's not much that can be done about sharks, but most of the microorganisms that are killing sea otters in California are a direct result of human activities. "There's no question that sea otters are getting bombarded with pollutants of all different kinds—chemical, biological, biotoxins—and horrific amounts of them," Miller said. And it is not uncommon for her to find evidence of several different parasites, pollutants, or toxins in just one animal. In fact, she told me, that's pretty much the rule. "And the tricky part," she said, "is figuring out which was the first domino to fall or how did all of those things result in the dead animal that's on my table."

Strangely enough, Miller's greatest worry of late is cat feces. A protozoan parasite called *Toxoplasma gondii* actively reproduces in a variety of wild and domestic cat species, and the cells of the parasite's eggs pass through the cat in its feces, where it is believed to survive in the environment for months or years. Researchers speculate that the parasite then makes its way to coastal waters when cat litter is flushed down the toilet or when heavy rains wash it into storm drains. Male sea otters in California have a 70 percent chance of being infected with it, an amazingly high rate given that the only known hosts are mountain lions, bobcats, and domestic cats. How the parasite gets into sea otters is uncertain, but it is probably absorbed by filter-feeding mollusks or consumed by snails as they graze on seaweed, and those animals are then eaten by otters. It has become such a grave issue that the bill that passed the California legislature in 2006 to establish the California Sea Otter Fund also included provisions requiring that packages of cat litter sold in the state be labeled with proper disposal methods to protect otters.

No one knows when *Toxoplasma* first began infecting sea otters. Nancy Thomas at the US Geological Survey's National Wildlife Health Center in Wisconsin was the first pathologist to examine sea otters in any detail back in the early 1990s, and she found it in some of the first animals she tested. Just because a large number of dead otters are infected with *Toxoplasma*, however, does not mean that it is responsible for killing the animals. Miller says it typically lingers in the background and has an indeterminate effect. But she calls the parasite "a great biological marker for the extent that sea otters get exposed to land-based pollution." That's her take-home message—abundant quantities of terrestrial pollutants are finding their way into the nearshore environment and sickening marine wildlife—and that message comes with a long list of other land-based pollutants that are also being found in dead sea otters, some of which are rather unusual.

For instance, dead sea otters are turning up with a brain disease typically found in horses, equine protozoal myeloencephalitis, which is caused by a single-celled parasite called *Sarcocystis neurona* that is very similar to the one that causes *Toxoplasma*. But *Sarcocystis* comes from the feces of opossums, which aren't even native to California. Miller said the two diseases are very similar. The only difference is one comes from cat feces and the other from opossum feces. *Sarcocystis*, which killed forty otters in Morro Bay in April 2004 following a large rainstorm that probably washed the parasite into the bay, tends to kill otters that feed primarily on clams and innkeeper worms, while *Toxoplasma* kills mostly snail-eating otters. But beyond that, little is known about either parasite's transmission.

In addition, Miller has found roundworms in sea otter brains that are almost certainly the same parasite found in raccoons, and she even discovered one case of an otter infected with a parasite that likely originated in a rat. And in 2007, she started seeing dead otters that appeared to be bright yellow in color; she eventually traced this to a freshwater toxin called microcystin that is commonly found in farm ponds. She later discovered that microcystin was being washed into the Pajaro River in Watsonville and flowing thirteen miles downstream to Monterey Bay. The first recorded case of an otter dying from the toxin occurred right at the mouth of the river.

The link between the land and sea is the most critical component of these sea otter deaths. Harbors, bays, and other locations where freshwater enters the marine environment accumulate a wide range of other nasty stuff, too, including effluent from wastewater treatment facilities, pesticides, industrial chemicals, and organic pollutants like PCBs, all of which have been found in sea otters. These areas tend to be high-risk sites for otter mortality. This land-sea link makes sea otters sentinels not only for the health of the coastal marine environment where they live, but also for the health of the terrestrial environment. And because these are all terrestrial pathogens and man-made pollutants, sea otters have little natural immunity to them.

Land-based pathogens aren't the only reasons that southern sea otters are getting sick, though. They're facing numerous marine factors as well, just like in Alaska, including domoic acid and paralytic shellfish poisoning, both of which are associated with algal blooms. Domoic acid, a neurotoxin, was first discovered to be a problem in 1998, when it caused a large number of sea lion deaths in California. It causes seizures in the animals, and they are often observed to vomit and behave like they are constantly itching. Humans who survive eating shellfish contaminated with domoic acid often experience memory loss. It is believed that the toxins from an algal bloom will get into fish first, followed by the sea lions that eat the infected fish. It takes a while before the toxin reaches the animals on the seafloor and those like sea otters who eat the benthic creatures. "I typically can set my watch and say, we've got sea lions coming in with domoic acid, so maybe a month from now we'll start seeing otters" with it, Miller said.

The one cause of death that just makes my head spin is mating trauma. Mating among sea otters is no romantic affair. It's a violent act that typically involves the male biting the female's nose. Just about every female otter of reproductive age has scars on her nose from this vicious behavior, and some have even had their nose ripped entirely off. The behavior is much more common among otters in California than in Alaska, so much so that otter biologist Jack Ames has joked that Alaska otters should be brought to California to introduce "gentleman genes" to the California population. While it's not unusual among Mustelid males to bite the neck or the nose during mating, southern sea otters tend to go a little overboard in their aggression. Unfortunately, open wounds on the nose are a portal of entry for bacteria and other organisms that cause infections that can often lead to death, especially when the injured otter may also be fighting off *Toxoplasma* or *Sarcocystis* or any of the other disease-causing microorganisms. Sometimes the injured nose will swell up, making it difficult for the animal to breathe and leading to problems in its lungs. There have even been documented cases where a male sea otter has actually drowned a female while mating.

According to Miller, it's not just female sea otters that are injured from aggressive males, however. Competition for females often leads male otters to bite other males. She said it is not uncommon to find scarring on the noses, paws, flippers, and testicles of male otters that almost certainly was caused by other males. And occasionally she has even found males whose baculum, or penis bone, was broken from a bite. "If you think about it, it's a pretty good strategy if you want to get Bob out of commission," she said. There are also records of male sea otters that have raped and killed harbor seal pups, which sounds almost like a made-up story in a tabloid newspaper but which Miller said "would not be classified as abnormal in the animal sense." (It still sounds pretty disturbing to me.) She pointed to Elkhorn Slough, an estuary off Monterey Bay where sea otters live amid a harbor seal rookery, as a site where such behavior probably takes place, where male otters with raging hormones are in close proximity to young seals that don't fight back.

The closer that Miller and others examine dead otters, the more pathogens and diseases they find. Two orphaned sea otter pups were discovered in 2014 to have a virus similar to chicken pox that causes skin lesions that result in fur loss. And the loss of fur is a great concern because, lacking a blubber layer, sea otters are likely to lose their natural insulation and become hypothermic, potentially leading to a quick death. And Miller is beginning to find an increase in mortality due to heart failure, though little is known yet about what may be causing it.

JUST ABOUT EVERY sea otter found dead along the California coastline eventually makes its way to Melissa Miller's laboratory, about 250 to 300 animals each year. Most of them arrive between March and early June, with another peak in September and October, but hardly a week goes by that she doesn't receive a couple dead otters. Sometimes they arrive by FedEx; sometimes they're hand carried by a state park or beach employee; sometimes they arrive in bulk and in various stages of decomposition. That means that about 10 percent of the southern sea otter population turns up at her pathology lab each year, which most estimates suggest probably represents about half of the total number of southern sea otters that die annually. Those that don't eventually make it to her necropsy table probably lived in the Big Sur area, where few people reside and where access to the coastline is limited.

Miller, whose early career path included jobs as a sea lion trainer, tire changer, chambermaid, and field biologist, describes her present job as "a medical examiner for wildlife." Her aim, she said, is to tell the story of every animal that arrives at her lab by not only trying to learn how it died, but also determining how it lived and how that relates to how it died. Freshly dead otters receive a full necropsy with tissue samples analyzed in great detail. But due to limited funding, those that have already begun to decompose are frozen and later thawed in batches to receive what Miller calls a "demo necropsy," an abbreviated examination that does not include the collection and testing of tissue samples. She conducts about one hundred detailed necropsies each year, a standardized procedure that takes about four hours to complete. "I don't care if there's a knife sticking out of it; we're going to do the exact same protocol all the way through the examination," she said. That's how she discovered that *Toxoplasma* was such a common source of infection in sea otters, by carefully examining every tissue of every animal for any factors that may have contributed to its death, regardless of whether a seemingly obvious cause of death was evident.

The female otter that was on Miller's stainless-steel table when Renay and I visited had clearly seen better days. It had been found dead of unknown causes on the shore at Palm Beach State Park in Watsonville two days earlier, and it had probably been dead at least two days before being found. Miller was determined to find out how the otter had died.

At first glance, the animal appeared to be in good physical shape, though its belly had already begun to bloat from the gases produced during the decomposition process. Judging by the otter's incomplete dentition, Miller said it was not yet one year old, but its eyes were bulging and blood filled, which immediately alerted Miller that it had likely experienced head trauma.

The necropsy process was much like what we observed in Kristin Worman's lab. But because of the otter's bulging eyes, Miller focused on skinning, probing, and closely examining the dead otter's head and skull for any other evidence of trauma, but none was found. No noticeable wounds were found after an examination of the animal's pelt and torso, either, so Miller's preliminary conclusion was that the animal's cause of death was probably something other than a gunshot. She then cut into the otter's body cavity. Bloated large intestines forced their way out, and very quickly the stench became overpowering—not like the smell of roadkill, an aroma I'm quite familiar with, but instead something slightly sweeter yet so potent that I repeatedly had to take a step away to blow out the putrid smells and attempt to breathe in cleaner air. I've observed enough dead and decomposing animals that the sight and smell of them seldom causes me to flinch, but the stench this time was overwhelming.

After examining the otter's major abdominal organs, Miller said the otter appeared to be in good physical shape, so trauma remained the most likely cause of death. She became even more confident of that assessment when she opened the chest cavity, unexpectedly revealing large quantities of pooled and clotted blood. "Now we know it's trauma, probably a boat strike," said Miller. "That would explain why it's in otherwise good physical condition." Using a large pair of pruning shears, she cut through the rib cage and observed even more blood, which she described as "severe hemorrhaging into the chest." She double-checked that there were no bullet wounds or holes, and found none, but went back to look again, still with a question in her mind about whether there could be a gunshot wound.

After another five minutes of carefully examining the inside of the pelt in the vicinity of the animal's chest and shining the overhead lights more effectively on the animal, she finally found a minuscule hole in the fur in the vicinity of the right side of the chest. It was so small that it couldn't have been made by typical-caliber ammunition. Instead, she considered that it may have been from a BB or shotgun pellet, perhaps a bullet fragment, or even a broken rib poking through the skin. "It's a very subtle hole," she said. So she made the decision to stop the procedure and do a "lead hunt" with a radiograph to determine if a bullet remained in the carcass.

When the X-rays were taken, they showed a single shotgun pellet lodged just above the tenth rib (of seventeen) on the left side of the body. Based on the hole in the pelt, Miller concluded that the projectile entered on the animal's right side, proceeded through the chest cavity, and lodged in the left side.

Miller said it was the first time she had seen a shotgun pellet cause the death of an otter, since most pellets bounce off of their dense fur or lodge in the fur. They seldom penetrate. She still didn't rule out that the animal had been shot and later struck in the head by a boat, but that would have to await further analysis.

"This is not a case we're going to solve," she said, "because you can't do ballistics on pellets. Without an eyewitness, the chance of finding the culprit is remote."

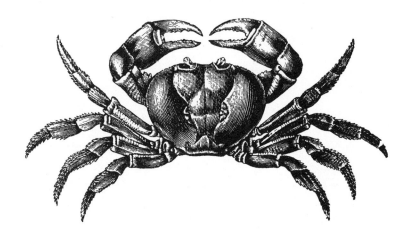

Chapter 8: Cucumbers and Geoducks

PRINCE OF WALES ISLAND, ALASKA

AFTER ALASKA attained statehood in 1959, it became responsible for the small sea otter populations in the state, and from 1965 to 1969, the Alaska Department of Fish and Game relocated 403 sea otters from the Aleutian Islands and Prince William Sound to six sites in Southeast Alaska: Cape Spencer (25 otters), Yakobi Island (30), Khaz Bay (194), Biorka Island (48), the Maurelle Islands (51), and the Barrier Islands (55). An unknown number was also reintroduced to Yakutat Bay just north of the region. Out of all those otters, just 106 survived the process and, along with their offspring, have spread throughout the outer coast of the region. Many continue to infiltrate the archipelago's nooks and crannies. Those 106 otters have multiplied into more than twenty-five thousand otters, according to a 2012 survey of the area, more than eight times as many as are found in all of California and a 12 percent annual growth rate that continues unabated.

Zac Hoyt, a doctoral student at the University of Alaska in Fairbanks, has spent nearly ten years studying the sea otter population in southern Southeast Alaska, and he has modeled the growth of the population in a variety of ways. He said that, unlike for sea otters in California and other parts of Alaska, there has been nothing to regulate the population of otters in the southeastern part of the state. Whereas sharks and killer whales are keeping the otter population in check elsewhere, the otters themselves are the apex predator in Southeast Alaska. The only limitation to the growth of the population is the availability of food, and so far there seems to be plenty. Hoyt also called Southeast Alaska's sea otters a "closed population," meaning that no sea otters are emigrating from other areas into the region, nor are sea otters from Southeast Alaska moving elsewhere. Their population is growing entirely through their own reproduction.

But Hoyt's model indicates that it isn't happening in a predictable manner. The sea otter population in southern Southeast Alaska has, in fact, grown in a herky-jerky way, with some areas experiencing rapid growth, others growing slowly and steadily, and still others seeing their once-abundant population crashing altogether. When the first organized sea otter survey of Southeast Alaska was conducted in 1975, the animals were found to have expanded their range from the initial release sites, but there wasn't much of a build-up in the population numbers. A few otters had reached as far north as Coronation Island, off the northwest coast of Prince of Wales Island, about thirty-five miles from the Maurelle Islands release site, but most had traveled much shorter distances. The next survey, in 1983, discovered that the range expansion in that area had slowed, but the density of animals in the places they were found had grown significantly. Five years later, biologists learned that the otters were on the move again, colonizing the Bay of Pillars and Sumner Island to the north and Lulu Island to the south. Population density increased again, too, with more than five times as many otters counted than just five years previously. Subsequent surveys had similar results, with range expansions and population densities speeding up and slowing down over time.

Some areas, however, showed unexpected results. Port Malmesbury on the west side of Kuiu Island, for instance, had the highest density of otters in all of southern Southeast Alaska in 2003, with about 470 animals recorded. But in the surveys of 2010 and 2011, when large areas of Southeast Alaska were being colonized by sea otters and otter numbers were growing rapidly, almost no otters were found in the Port Malmesbury area. And the population at Coronation Island has also experienced a significant decrease in otter numbers recently. Something appears to be limiting population growth in some areas, most likely the availability of food. "It looks like the otters may have overshot the carrying capacity that the habitat can withstand," Hoyt said. "It's a dynamic seen in other sea otter populations as well." It's having a dramatic effect on the entire ecosystem and on the economic health of the region, too.

Like in other areas of their range, when sea otters were extirpated from Southeast Alaska during the fur trade, the species the otters preyed upon flourished, including sea urchins, Dungeness crab, and sea cucumbers. And when fishermen discovered a market in the Far East for some of those species, commercial fisheries became established. The return of sea otters to the region, which many consider a tremendous conservation success, has been met with considerable anger among the vocal fishermen, who rightly fear competing with sea otters for shellfish.

In the 1990s, fishermen in Southeast Alaska harvested as many as four million pounds a year of red sea urchins, packaging their roe for shipment to Japan. A regional urchin management plan directed that just 6 percent of the urchins in the region be harvested each year to ensure that the fishery remained sustainable. But an unregulated commercial fishery for urchins along the Pacific coast of Russia over the last fifteen years flooded the market, and an influx of sea otters has decimated the Southeast Alaska urchin population, so the Alaska fishery is no longer as robust as it once was, declining to about half a million pounds per year in 2014. "I don't really see the urchin fishery recovering," said Phil Doherty, director of the Southeast Alaska Regional Dive Fisheries Association, "and the reason is the sea otters."

He's right. According to Hoyt and his University of Alaska colleague Ginny Eckert, when sea otters recolonize an area, their preferred prey is red sea urchins. While Hoyt's studies of the diet of sea otters in southern Southeast Alaska found that the animals ate sixty-eight different prey species, in the first few years after otters returned to an area, 99 percent of their diet consisted of red sea urchins. "Urchins are an amazing food for otters," said Hoyt. "They're easy to get, it doesn't take them a lot of effort, they don't have to search very hard for them, they break them open easily, and the roe provides them with a great deal of energy." As a result, he added, about ten to fifteen years after otters move into an area, commercial fisheries for sea urchins are no longer viable.

When the urchin fishery crashed in Southeast Alaska—like the commercial abalone fishery before it, which was wiped out due to overfishing—most of the fishermen simply shifted their focus to harvesting other species. Many switched to giant red sea cucumbers, a slow-moving, spiny slug-like creature that feeds on detritus on the seafloor. Sea cucumbers have five longitudinal muscles running along their body that fishermen slice off after harvest for sale to Japan, and the remaining skin is then dried and sold to China. Launched in 1981, the sea cucumber fishery now includes about two hundred dive fishermen in Southeast Alaska who harvest nearly 1.5 million pounds of sea cucumbers per year.

These commercially harvested species live from the intertidal zone down to several hundred feet deep and are caught not with traditional fishing gear but simply by picking them up by hand from the seafloor or digging for them while diving beneath the surface. Which is exactly how sea otters harvest them. And the otters are much more efficient at it than people and completely unregulated.

The sea cucumber fishery is looking like it may be the next to crash. While people, otters, and otter prey seemed to live in balance and harmony prior to the marine fur trade, that does not appear possible any longer if the prey species are targeted for commercial harvest and the otters are protected from harm. Fishermen who harvest geoducks (pronounced "gooey ducks"), the world's largest burrowing clam, haven't begun to feel the effects of the growing sea otter population much yet, but they know their time will come.

Geoducks live in coastal areas of the Pacific Northwest and northward to Alaska, where they grow to about ten inches and can weigh more than seven pounds. Found buried up to three feet deep in muddy and sandy bottom habitats of bays and estuaries, they live for well over one hundred years, feeding on single-celled marine algae and other microorganisms that they filter out of the water with a siphon that can extend nearly forty inches to the surface of the seafloor.

Dive fishing is a dangerous business, and diving for geoducks is especially hard work, which is why the sea otters haven't had much of an impact on the fishery yet. The otters eat the easy prey first, like the urchins and sea cucumbers that live on the surface of the seafloor. But the challenging work of unearthing geoducks is worth it to the fishermen. It's a lucrative business harvesting geoducks for sale to markets in China, Hong Kong, and Vietnam. Most fishermen earn about $75,000 per year working just one day per week for six months each year (though to enter the business they have to buy a fishing permit that cost about $90,000 in 2014). And they're beginning to get worried about their future.

TO GET AN IDEA of what the dive fishermen in Southeast Alaska are facing from the influx of sea otters, I spent a morning with Kathy Peavey, a glass artist, photographer, and entrepreneur who occasionally joins her husband, Matt, on the *Anne Louise*, their dive-fishing vessel. When she's not making art or serving as a deckhand, she ferries the media and others around the local waters to show them the challenges the expanding number of sea otters are creating for the fishermen in the area. I met her at North Cove Harbor in the town of Craig on Prince of Wales Island, home to the majority of the dive-fishing fleet on the island, perhaps twenty repurposed boats of various sizes and shapes.

We slowly pulled out of the harbor, past an anonymous building where E. C. Phillips and Son buys most of the sea cucumbers and geoducks the fishermen harvest, and out into Klawock Inlet. In the summer, the inlet is usually filled with the noise and congestion of floatplanes coming and going, delivering cargo, visitors, and locals to points far and wide. We were greeted there by a small flock of rhinoceros auklets, gray seabirds with large orange beaks and white facial plumes. Peavey called them "king salmon ducks" for their propensity to show up in abundance just when the king salmon arrive in the region.

Peavey said that sea otters are just beginning to move into the immediate vicinity of Craig, but not far away on the fishing grounds the animals are already competing directly with the dive fishermen. We headed south and west a few miles, past the line that delineates the boundary of the Haida tribal territory in the south from the Tlingit lands to the north, and beyond Fish Egg Island, where salmon are known to spawn, on our way to Bucareli Bay, one of several designated geoduck and sea cucumber fishing grounds in the area. According to Peavey, the site on the southeast corner of San Fernando Island was colonized the year before after the otters expanded from the west side of the island. She said the animals "ate themselves out" of their previous site—also a designated dive-fishing ground—and have moved in to Bucareli Bay. They were easy for us to find.

The waters were surprisingly calm as we skirted the coast, but gray skies suggested that it wasn't going to stay that way for long. As we approached Balandra Island and a large kelp bed nearby, otters began appearing nearly everywhere we looked. A group of seven otters abruptly dived nearly in unison as we approached, while a solitary individual a hundred yards away hardly took notice of us. Several others lazily sank beneath the surface to avoid the noise of our boat, and one just stared contentedly at us without moving.

"Otters are invasive species around here; they're the rats of the sea," Peavey said. "It's just like an infestation of rats in New York City. You have to eradicate them or else the humans are going to lose—to the otters, the whales, the sea lions, and the wolves. We're going to lose our dive fisheries, and we can't afford to."

Peavey grew up in Oregon and came to Alaska to work in the fishing industry as a college student. She settled in Craig twenty-eight years ago. She acknowledges the importance of marine conservation and says she and her husband have no desire to wipe out otters entirely. But she is convinced that otters must be actively managed and their population reduced if the local communities are going to survive. In addition to the otters' effects on the commercial fishery, she worries that as the animals get closer to the villages, "you can kiss your subsistence fishing goodbye, too." She also points out that the kelp beds throughout the area are healthy and abundant and "don't need the otters to save the ecosystem." She appears to be right. During our three hours traveling on the water, large patches of living kelp were nearly always visible, including in areas where Peavey said otters had arrived only months previously, so the animals apparently weren't necessary to the maintenance of the kelp beds.

When we arrived at the San Fernando fishing grounds, no otters were visible, but Peavey was sure they were around nearby. Bad weather was forecast, and she said the otters know when storms are on the way, so they were probably in protected spots in the vicinity. And besides, she pointed out, we had just seen close to two dozen otters less than a mile away, an easy commute for a sea otter.

To the uninitiated, this stretch of coastline doesn't look much different from almost everywhere else you look nearby—steep rocky shores topped by tall spruces and cedars, rimmed by alders and crab apples, and at nearly every turn a bald eagle or three perched in a tree or on a pile of rocks. The divers work the sandy seafloor from thirty to seventy feet deep to collect geoducks, and harder-bottomed areas are scoured for sea cucumbers.

We headed north again along the eastern shore of San Fernando Island, past a Styrofoam buoy blown in from the 2012 Japanese tsunami, toward Eleven Mile Pass, a dive-fishing destination between the northern shore of the island and western shore of Prince of Wales Island. Again we found no otters on the fishing grounds, which surprised Peavey. Pointing out another patch of kelp, she said that the fishermen harvest the kelp as part of the regulated herring fishery. They entrap the herring in a seine net, hang kelp fronds into the seine, and wait for the fish to spawn on the kelp, at which time the fish are released and the fishermen collect the fish eggs for sale to Japan. "We accept the rules and the management plans for all these species, and the state manages them well to conserve the resource," she said. "We just need a similar management plan for the otters or it's all going to go to waste."

Peavey nodded toward the Maurelle Islands in the distance, one of the sites where the state successfully reintroduced sea otters in 1968, then turned to circle tiny Rosary Island, noting a spot where dive fishermen Stephanie and Brad Jurries are known to fish for geoducks.

THE DAY BEFORE my tour with Peavey, I met Stephanie Jurries at a public meeting for stakeholders seeking to discuss sea otter–related issues in Southeast Alaska, but she was the only commercial fisherman to attend. While most of the meeting dealt with the concerns of the Alaska Native communities, she held her own in articulating how otters were affecting her industry. While her husband dives for geoducks, Stephanie is a licensed sea cucumber fisherman, something she pursued after working in a coffee shop and fish processing plant. She paid $7,000 in 2007 for her commercial permit to harvest sea cucumbers, and she feels lucky she got into it when she did, since a permit cost $30,000 in 2014. She says that cucumber picking is easy, especially compared to harvesting geoducks.

"You just swim around and pick them up," Stephanie said. "There's a lot involved, but I was able to pick it up pretty quick." When she's on the seafloor collecting cucumbers, a two-hundred-foot air hose tethers her to a twenty-one-foot landing craft that her husband maneuvers to follow her progress. When she fills a bag with cucumbers, he drops down a line that she secures to the full bag, and he hauls it up. Then he drops down an empty bag and she continues picking.

The cucumber harvest season runs for about eight weeks beginning in October and takes place only on Mondays from 8:00 a.m. to 3:00 p.m. and on Tuesdays from 8:00 a.m. to 12:00 p.m. Each fisherman is limited to harvesting two thousand pounds of cucumbers each week, which Jurries said most fishermen used to be able to collect in a couple hours on Monday, but now it takes most fishermen until Tuesday morning. The state manages the sea cucumber population by collecting data on the harvest every Thursday during the fishing season and opening or closing particular fishing grounds depending on the health of the cucumber population.

According to Ginny Eckert, sea cucumbers may be the best-managed fishery in Alaska because the state Department of Fish and Game surveys the population on a regular basis, enabling it to make decisions about how many cucumbers can be sustainably harvested from week to week. "It takes a lot of work to find cucumbers these days," said Jurries. "We actually run around in a skiff with an underwater video camera to do survey work just to find them. The fishing grounds for cucumbers are changing, and it's all because of the otters."

While that's not entirely true, she's not far off. The frequent state surveys of sea cucumbers have enabled Eckert and other researchers to separate the effect that sea otters have on the sea cucumber population from that of the fishermen, something that cannot be done with any other fishery. Based on examinations of data as far back as 1994, when the state surveys began, Eckert said that "the impact of the otters is a function of time. The longer the otters have been there, the larger their impact is." In areas that sea otters recolonized prior to the beginning of the surveys, sea cucumbers are almost entirely absent, whereas in areas only recently recolonized, cucumbers are present but declining in number. Wondering if something besides sea otters could account for the decline, Eckert conducted a similar analysis of cucumber populations in areas where sea otters have not yet returned. She found slight declines in cucumber numbers during the sixteen-year span of the survey, up to about 20 percent in some areas, but nothing like the 100 percent drop in longtime otter zones. "It's a pretty impressive relationship," said Eckert. "Where we have no otters we have a much higher density of cucumbers, and as they colonize the area longer we see much lower and lower abundances of sea cucumbers." So even though sea cucumbers aren't the most preferred prey item of sea otters—they make up only about 13 percent of the otters' diet—the sea otters still drive cucumber populations to near extirpation over time. And, according to Eckert's study, commercial dive fishing has little or no effect on the density of sea cucumbers in Southeast Alaska.

What does that mean for sea cucumber fishermen like Stephanie Jurries? She knows that it's just a matter of time before she has to change careers. And in the meantime, she said it's a challenge to keep up with the changing cucumber populations from one place to another. One of her favorite places to dive for sea cucumbers was a place appropriately—or not—called Sea Otter Sound, which was finally closed to dive fishing in 2010. "The last day that I dove there, I was literally diving with the sea otters as they were eating cucumbers beside me," she said. "The next time that place was scheduled to open, it was immediately closed because there was no viable fishery left. There were just too many otters in the area." She said that is happening again and again throughout the region and forcing her to travel farther away to fish. "Fish and Game has all this survey data to figure out the sustainable level of harvest for the fishery, but they can't account for the fact that the otters are moving in and eating everything. One area that was going to have a seventy-thousand-pound quota was closed because the otters ate them all, and another place had a forty-thousand-pound quota that was cut to seventeen thousand pounds, which is so little that nobody even went there. The otters are changing our entire season."

Strangely enough, Jurries's opinion of sea otters started out much like that of most nonfishermen. "I was just like everybody else—I thought otters were cute and fuzzy," she said. "And they still are. But like anything else, they need to be managed properly. Everybody's hands are tied now because the Marine Mammal Protection Act is prohibiting people like me from hunting them. They need to manage otters like they would any other wildlife population. That's all that needs to happen."

ALL OF THE FISHERMEN in the region seem to agree about one thing: if sea otters are not "managed," the future of their fisheries is in jeopardy. They're probably right. Most of the biologists I spoke with agree that commercial shellfisheries and a healthy sea otter population in Southeast Alaska may be mutually exclusive. But, sadly, the kind of sea otter management the fishermen seek is lethal. They want large numbers of sea otters killed. That's happened before, of course, during the maritime fur trade two centuries ago, an event that most people today condemn for nearly driving sea otters to extinction. What did we learn from that experience? That unless all of the otters are killed, they are going to quickly repro-duce and recolonize wherever food is available. So killing a portion of the sea otter population isn't likely to resurrect the fisheries, at least not for long.

For more than one hundred years, a similar effort against coyotes has been undertaken throughout much of the American West. Millions of coyotes have been killed to prevent them from preying on sheep and other domestic livestock, and after all that, the population of coyotes is healthier than ever. Because as coyotes are killed, new territories become available for other coyotes to populate, and reproduction rates increase to fill those niches where abundant food resources are available. Sea otters have already proven that they are able to grow their population at a rapid rate to recolonize their historic range. Killing a segment of the population under the guise of "management" will just allow them to demon-strate that they can do it all over again.

Jim Curland of Friends of the Sea Otter calls the kind of man-agement that the fishermen have in mind "predator control," which is an illegal form of wildlife management when it comes to sea otters. Yet the fishermen's fear for their livelihood is real, and I cer-tainly don't blame them for seeking out whatever means they can to keep their industries afloat. To make their case, the Southeast Alaska Regional Dive Fisheries Association commissioned a report on the economic impact of sea otters on the fisheries. Called the McDowell Report for the consultants who conducted the study in 2011 (which was a follow-up to a similar report in 2005), it claims that sea otter predation on sea cucumbers, geoducks, sea urchins, and Dungeness crabs cost the Southeast Alaska economy as much as $28.3 million between 1995 and 2011. The authors say that sea otters in the region ate 3.2 million pounds of sea cucumbers from 1996 to 2011, 3.1 million pounds of red sea urchins from 1995 to 2005, 2.7 million pounds of Dungeness crabs from 2000 to 2010, and half a million pounds of geoducks from 2005 to 2011. The report concluded: "In short, commercial dive fishing and large populations of sea otters cannot coexist in the same waters. In addition, once the commercially viable biomass of crab and macroinvertebrates—such as sea cucumbers and geoducks—is gone, it likely will not return given sustained sea otter predation."

You'd be hard pressed to find anyone to disagree with that conclusion, including that last line. In 2013, the dive fishery association asked the state to survey areas that were closed to sea cucumber harvesting in 2001, to see if the population had rebounded, and there were hardly any cucumbers to be found. So it is unlikely that the fisheries will rebound unless the sea otter population crashes.

But not everyone agrees with other aspects of the McDowell Report, especially when it is put into the context of other economic realities. Rick Sinnott, for instance, a retired biologist with the Alaska Department of Fish and Game, wrote in the *Alaska Dispatch News* that a report commissioned by the Alaska Wilderness League found that nonresident visitors spent $360 million in Southeast Alaska in 2010 and 2011, and 42 percent of that spending was on observing wildlife, primarily viewing charismatic species like sea otters. He noted that the economic value of wildlife viewing to the region was "89 times the payroll generated by sea urchins, geoducks, and other marine invertebrates harvested by dive fishermen." Compared to the number of salmon and herring fishermen who would benefit from a healthier kelp ecosystem that sea otters provide, and the potential economic benefit to the region in the form of ecotourism and wildlife viewing, the decline of the dive fisheries over the next decade may not affect the region's economy as badly as many fear, at least not over the long term. But try telling the dive fishermen that.

Other elements are impacting commercial dive fisheries as well. Biologists speculate that the decline of sea cucumbers in areas that have not been colonized by sea otters may be due to any number of changes to the ecosystem or environmental conditions, like ocean acidification, as a result of the changing climate. No studies have been conducted as of yet to identify the causes of those declines, but it is clear that otters are not the culprit. "Other things are going on in the fishery besides just otters," said former Fish and Wildlife Service otter biologist Verena Gill, "but you wouldn't think so talking to the fishermen." The geoduck fishery is also facing issues unrelated to sea otters. During the 2013–14 season, the fishery came to an abrupt stop when customers in China—which represents about 99 percent of its market—found some clams contaminated by paralytic shellfish poisoning. Although the toxin does not harm the shellfish, it can be lethal to humans. When the fishermen tried to sell their product to Taiwan instead, the state of Alaska conducted tests of the geoducks, found the toxin, and shut down the fishery. "There's no doubt that sea otters consume a huge amount of what they [the fishermen] fish for, but they've got more going on in their industry than sea otters," Gill said.

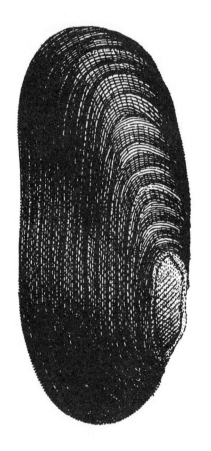

A southern sea otter in California waters, drying its hands

TOP: *A raft of southern sea otters in California*
BOTTOM: *Twin pups, a rarity, resting on their mother in Monterey Bay*

A California sea otter wrapped in kelp for stabilization

A young adult male challenges a mature male for territory in California

TOP: *An otter on land near Elkhorn Slough in California*
BOTTOM: *A mother shares a mussel with her growing pup in California*

TOP: *California sea otters haul out on land*
BOTTOM: *Northern sea otters holding hands in Kenai Fjords National Park, Alaska*

TOP: *A northern sea otter feeds on a mussel in Kenai Fjords National Park, Alaska*
BOTTOM: *A California sea otter surfaces after a dive in Morro Bay, California*

TOP: *Otters on an iceberg in Harriman Fjord in Prince William Sound, Alaska*
BOTTOM: *Adult northern sea otters with pup in foreground in Prince William Sound*

Chapter 9: Significantly Altered

WHILE THE DIVE fishermen in Southeast Alaska seem anxious to see the region's sea otter population exterminated, the opinion about sea otters among Native Alaskans isn't much better. That's because the otters are making it more and more difficult for tribal members to find the traditional foods they are used to harvesting from coastal areas to feed their families. "What the sea otters like is what we like—crabs, sea cucumbers, sea urchins, clams," said Mike Jackson, who works for the Organized Village of Kake, a federally recognized tribe on Kupreanof Island, centrally located on the Alaska panhandle. "Sea otters have surrounded our village now. There are pods of fifty to three hundred that hang out together. They're wiping out our customary traditional foods."

At the mouth of Gunnuk Creek and Little Gunnuk Creek in Kake, for instance, where a wide tidal flat allows tribal members to drive onto the beach to dig for butter clams, cockles, and littlenecks, sea otters have moved in and absconded with the bulk of the harvest. "They're really sneaky," Jackson said. "They come in with the tide, and you can hear them using their little hammers opening the clams when the town is quiet at nighttime. We usually harvest thousands of pounds for ourselves for the winter, but now we have to scratch to get any."

It's the same story one hundred miles to the south in Klawock, a predominantly Native community on Prince of Wales Island, where families used to harvest sea cucumbers, clams, and cockles to share with tribal members. When Dennis Nickerson was a young boy, he harvested shellfish with his family at nearby San Cristobal Channel and Cruz Pass. "That's how we practiced our system of bartering," he said. "It's one of our more common practices that we still use to this day, something we handed down from generation to generation. That's how we made sure our families were fed; it's done on a community basis."

But the sea otters have made that practice more difficult.

"It's been a while since I've harvested shellfish on our side of the island because the areas we used to go to just have empty shells on the shoreline," said Nickerson, a Tlingit member of the Prince of Wales Island Tribal Sea Otter Commission. "We sat on the beach in silence a while back, and all we could hear was the sound of otters pounding shellfish on a rock. They were decimating the area. There's barely anything left."

It's a story that Sonia Ibarra has heard again and again from Native Alaskans up and down the coast of Southeast Alaska. A doctoral student at the University of Alaska at Fairbanks, she is interviewing Alaska Natives from throughout the region to document how sea otters are affecting the harvest of subsistence foods, capturing memories of how earlier generations coexisted with sea otters, and mapping the sites where families harvested clams and other foods before sea otters returned to the area.

"There is a lot of consensus that people are having a hard time harvesting important foods that they've harvested for a long time, foods that are an important part of their nutritional intake,"

Ibarra said. She's hoping her study will identify how to balance the needs of people and sea otters, and she has received a wide variety of suggestions.

Ibarra believes that the best idea so far is to use a kind of marine spatial planning to define areas where subsistence harvesting is productive and convenient, and attempt to keep otters from those locations—by hunting or other means—while allowing otters to freely use other areas. "It's the same idea as traditional stories I've heard, how people coexisted with sea otters in the past," said Ibarra. "The really productive shellfish areas, close to villages, were for people to harvest, and outside that area was designated for sea otters."

How that would be accomplished is another story. The California effort to declare a no-otter zone was an expensive failure, since it's nearly impossible to keep otters from going where they want to go. Until this or any other strategy is implemented, however, local Natives will remain frustrated and angry that little has been done to resolve the issue to their satisfaction. And they lay most of the blame on the federal government and the Marine Mammal Protection Act.

The legislation is contentious throughout the region, though most residents would agree that its intent is admirable—to protect whales, dolphins, seals, polar bears, and other marine mammals, including sea otters, from being killed or harassed in US waters. One way it does this is by prohibiting the possession or importation of marine mammals or any parts of them. That means not only is it illegal to acquire a living or dead marine mammal, it is also illegal to possess a seal skull, walrus tusk, polar bear pelt, or any other body part without a permit. And permits are very hard to come by.

Coastal Alaska Natives are exempt from the legislation, however, thanks to former Alaska senator Ted Stevens, who advocated for the exemption in an effort to recognize the traditional use of marine mammals by Native Alaskans. It allows them to hunt and kill as many sea otters as they wish at any time of year, as long as the animal is used for subsistence consumption or to create authentic Native clothing or handicrafts. And the exemption applies even to Natives who don't live anywhere near the range of the sea otter. Natives from Barrow, 1,100 miles away, for instance, can travel to the Aleutians or to Southeast Alaska to hunt sea otters if they wish. Stevens justified the exemption so as not to "wipe out the Eskimo culture and several important Native handicraft activities in the process."

The makers of traditional handicrafts are allowed to sell their products to anyone they wish as well, which is why—despite the prohibition on owning marine mammal parts—it isn't illegal to purchase seal skin gloves, sea otter–fur hats, or other garments or jewelry made from marine mammal fur, teeth, or bone. But the exemption comes with a complicated set of rules that can be interpreted in many ways, which has annoyed a large number of Natives seeking to maintain their tribal traditions. And it has even landed a few in jail. Their anger spilled over in 2014 at a public meeting to discuss the implications of the growing sea otter population and the rules imposed by the legislation.

IN A RAMSHACKLE community hall in Klawock, where a group of sea otter biologists, a couple fishermen, and a large number of Tlingit and Haida Natives from throughout Southeastern Alaska gathered, tensions rose quickly. The meeting's agenda—which was planned largely by Nickerson and the Organized Village of Kasaan, a tribal government a few miles away—was designed as an opportunity for otter experts to share what they had learned about otters in the region in an effort to respond to concerns that the abundant animals were wiping out the commercial and traditional harvesting of marine invertebrates. I watched as speakers from the US Fish and Wildlife Service, University of Alaska, and other agencies made brief presentations, followed by a panel discussion of scientists from California and British Columbia, who were invited to share their experience managing sea otter reintroductions and range expansions in their areas. But things didn't quite proceed as planned.

The meeting got testy when representatives of the Fish and Wildlife Service—the agency most of the Natives view as the bad guy in the battle over sea otters and shellfish—tried to report how many otters were believed to live in the area. Questions and comments from the assemblage began almost immediately, and for almost ninety minutes a microphone was passed among the audience members. Few had questions, and those who did were not expecting answers. Most wanted to tell their personal stories of how their favorite shellfishing site had been rapidly depleted by otters, or how federal otter regulations were interfering with their traditional practices, or how they felt excluded from the process of establishing the regulations, or how a neighbor was entrapped by law enforcement and arrested for breaking the rules. Several comments expressed displeasure with the entire rulemaking process, including some that were directed at the tribes' inability to figure out what to do next. And a few people made broad comments about oppression and a desire to pursue their traditional ways without government interference. One speaker declared the Marine Mammal Protection Act "broken," while another announced that it was "time to amend" the legislation. Still another said that the legislation meant that "sea otters have more rights than we do, the sovereign indigenous people."

The intensity and passion of the speakers caught me somewhat off guard, though I had been warned that it wasn't going to be an easy meeting to attend. It opened my eyes to perspectives I had read about—Native American oppression, chief among them—but which I had wrongfully assumed were mostly a thing of the past. So I sat quietly and tried to put myself in their shoes to better understand their concerns.

All of those who commented appeared heartfelt and sincere. And I was impressed with their ability to laugh and chat with the targets of their hostility, despite their displeasure with the situation, during breaks in the daylong proceedings. They appeared to know that the government representatives in the room weren't responsible for the rules, so they had no personal animosity toward them. But that did not make them any less angry.

One of the primary targets of the speakers was the Marine Mammal Protection Act's rules determining which Native Alaskans are allowed to hunt sea otters. Since the animals were absent from the region prior to the last few decades, older members of the tribes did not grow up hunting otters. But it didn't take them long to learn after sea otters moved back into the area. Mike Jackson, for instance, who has hunted seals for most of his life, began hunting sea otters in the 1980s, and now he is teaching his grandson to hunt. He is one of about fifteen otter hunters in Kake. In some of the larger communities, however, some Natives who want to hunt sea otters are prohibited from doing so. That's because only those whose ancestry is at least one-quarter Native Alaskan can participate in the hunt. And as more and more Natives marry non-Natives, it means that it is increasingly difficult for tribal traditions—like sea otter hunting—to be passed on to the next generation. It means it is illegal for many fathers to take their sons hunting.

PETER WILLIAMS isn't facing that obstacle. His father was a full-blooded Yupik, and although Williams was raised by his non-Native mother in Tlingit territory and struggled at times with his identity, he eventually developed a close connection to his Native roots. Even at a young age, he found peace in participating in subsistence activities like fishing and sharing his catch with the community. Later he worked a trapline and learned to hunt seals with a friend, but it wasn't a practice that came easy to him.

"It was a long journey for me to be able to hunt," said Williams, who is well known in the area as a hunter and known far beyond Alaska for the fashions he makes from sea otter pelts. "I would talk to people who hunted, and I'd go out and experiment, but I always felt really bad. I had a hard time taking an animal's life."

By studying his ancestors' hunting rituals, however, Williams saw how sea otter hunting could be a spiritual journey of self-discovery, one he said is "the most Alaska Native thing I can do." That journey begins days before he actually picks up his rifle, as he monitors the weather and tides, pays attention to his mental and physical state, and packs his gear in preparation for the hunt. "One of the things I really like about hunting is that everything is a ritual, everything is to be appreciated," he said.

At home in Sitka on the night before a hunt, as he finalizes his preparations, Williams announces his intentions, telling the animals what he plans to do and why. In the morning, he performs a spiritual smudging ritual using a plant called Labrador tea; he describes the ritual as somewhat like the Catholic Church's use of incense, waving smoke from the smoldering leaves over his body and rifle, cleansing himself while praying for his own safety and praying that his kills are quick. He finds this ritual helps him tap into his intuition, allowing him to be more successful at finding animals to hunt.

Usually hunting alone, Williams cruises around in his boat looking for a group of sea otters, avoiding females with pups and preferring subadult males, which he claims are easier to hunt. When he finds his prey, he stops at the nearest islet and, from a standing position, rests his .223 rifle on a life jacket placed on the rocks, and waits for the animals to come within range.

"In my head, I ask for its life and squeeze the trigger," he said.

Williams hunts year-round, since the quality of a sea otter's fur doesn't fluctuate seasonally, but he tends to hunt less during the short winter days when the weather is windy. Some days he is successful and some days he isn't. On his best day, he killed eleven sea otters, and in his most successful year he harvested seventy-eight. But he said he takes only what he needs, which he thinks is a concept that non-Native hunters targeting deer and geese, facing hunting seasons and bag limits, find hard to understand.

When he does hunt and is successful, he collects the animal's floating carcass and performs one last ritual, one based on a traditional Yupik seal-hunting practice that he read about. He offers the sea otter its last drink of water. Williams said the ritual originates from the belief that, since seals spend their entire life in salt water, they must be very thirsty. And if hunters give the animal its last drink of water, the seal will give its life to them and its spirit will return.

Williams offers sea otters their last drink of water from the same water bottle he drinks from himself. "For me, it's the moment of saying thanks and recognizing that water is an important key to life," he said. "I take that moment and share something that's precious to me and precious to all life, including this animal that just gave itself for me. It's a moment to say thank-you and to make peace."

THE OTHER IMPORTANT rule Native Alaskans must follow to legally hunt sea otters is that they must affix a Fish and Wildlife Service tag to the animal's skull and hide within thirty days to help track the carcasses that are legally harvested. Commercial tanners are not allowed to process a hide without a tag. Tanning is an expensive process, costing more than $100 per pelt, and with the added cost of shipping the pelts to distant tanneries and paying for the cost of ammunition and boat fuel, sea otter hunting is an expensive activity. It's one reason why few Alaska Natives hunt otters. And it's why many Natives supported legislation proposed by Alaska state senator Bert Stedman that would have paid a $100 bounty for every sea otter killed.

"At $1.50 per bullet, you have to be a pretty good hunter to stay a hunter," said Mike Jackson. "I would have really liked that bounty, because it would have afforded a lot of local people to go hunt sea otter. It would be nice if we had some kind of incentive for people who are almost able to go hunting but can't afford to buy gas and bullets. That's who would benefit most from a bounty."

The concept of a bounty, however, is unappealing to most people, who view it as a crude wildlife-management tactic better left in the past. It also appeared to some people that it was an illegal predator-control strategy devised to reduce sea otter numbers to accommodate the demands of commercial fishermen and a way of going behind the backs of the government biologists who are charged with assessing and managing the sea otter population for the benefit of all.

At the public meeting I attended, while several attendees shared unhappiness with the rules and regulations for sea otter hunting, the issue the assemblage spoke about most vehemently involved the definition and interpretation of the simple phrase "significantly altered." It's a key phrase in the Marine Mammal Protection Act for those seeking to turn a tanned sea otter pelt into a traditional product that can be sold to non-Natives. That's because Native Alaskans are not allowed to sell sea otter pelts to non-Natives without significantly altering them into traditional handicrafts or other products like hats, gloves, teddy bears, and quilted blankets. The Marine Mammal Protection Act exemption was intended to allow Native Alaskans to continue their traditional practices, which included making ceremonial garb and other items from sea otter pelts. According to a Fish and Wildlife Service pamphlet, a pelt is considered significantly altered when it is no longer recognizable as a whole sea otter hide and it is substantially changed by weaving, carving, stitching, sewing, lacing, beading, drawing, painting, or being made into another material.

It took three long days of meetings with Native hunters and artisans throughout coastal Alaska to come up with that definition. But it hasn't appeased hunters who want to sell unaltered pelts or those who make handicrafts and think the rules allow non-Native wildlife managers to judge the quality of their artistry.

"It's telling us what we can and can't do with our indigenous commerce," said Nickerson, noting that the rules require handicraft techniques in use before 1972 when the legislation passed. "It's basically telling us that we can't adapt our commerce; we have to hold on to our ancestral methods." It was only recently that Native artisans were allowed to use zippers, for instance, because they weren't considered traditional.

Jackson and many others who make high-end handicrafts, like clothing, hats, and purses, don't object to the significantly altered rule. He said that it takes a great deal of work to make a pelt into something that has "value and uniqueness" and will sell in his shop. But others raised their voices at the meeting and facetiously wondered how many stitches or beads are enough to significantly alter a pelt.

Later, Peter Williams told me that the language is problematic to him as well. "If I shoot an animal in the head and take its skin off its body, does it get any more significantly altered than that?" he asked. He recognizes the need for the rules, but "as someone who is a cultural bearer, I get hesitant and skeptical when someone is trying to define what culture and art is, especially someone outside of the culture. . . . I think it's problematic when an agency that's outside of my culture tells me what is or isn't my culture and what art is and isn't, especially when culture and art evolve by their very nature."

THE HANDICRAFTS THAT Williams makes have no problem passing the significantly altered test. He considers himself a fashion designer and vests, skirts, hats, and other garments made under his label Shaman Furs were featured in a runway show at Fashion

Week Brooklyn in 2016. He has also been an artist in residence at the Santa Fe Art Institute, lectured at Yale University, and demonstrated skin sewing techniques at various venues.

He said the process of designing and making his handicrafts "just feels right and important to me. . . . It furthers my connection with the animal, which I think is at the core. It's about connection and intimacy and having this relationship with the animal. The more I'm connected with the animal, the more I work and create and celebrate with it, the more I get to know it and myself and my culture."

When he receives an otter pelt from the tannery, he sprays it with water, stretches it, and staples it on a board to get rid of wrinkles and to give him as much material to work with as possible. He then draws his pattern on the hide, cuts it out with a razor blade, and uses a leather needle and upholstery thread to sew the fur by hand. He said that hand sewing feels cathartic and meditative, and it reflects the traditional methods his ancestors used.

Williams learned to sew otter fur by reading books, experimenting on his own, and asking furriers and Native artisans about their techniques. That's also how he learned to design fashions, and his designs continue to reflect the lessons he learned from his mentors. He has been pleased to find that many elements he learned about the design and construction of garments, many of which were based on Italian designs, are reflected in traditional Native-made garments as well. "I pick up things from everywhere, and somehow it leaps back to my ancestry in some weird way," he said.

Given the expense of hunting, tanning, and constructing his fashions, Williams's designs aren't cheap. So his customers are primarily people with considerable disposable income, especially those with a strong connection with sea otters, most often those who had a powerful experience seeing them in the wild. But that customer base is somewhat narrow, so he's finding it a challenge to make a living. After five years of working at it full time, he's still in the red. But the visibility and recognition he is finally receiving at fashion shows, on the internet, and at other events make him feel hopeful that his career is about to take off. Unfortunately, the increased interest of other Native Alaskans in making handicrafts is driving prices down. He has never before seen so many otter-fur handicrafts at craft fairs in Alaska. So Williams is focusing his attention on the higher-end fashion scene on the East Coast.

"Having my own business is pretty hard, and trying to share and talk about something that's new and unheard of and has controversy around it is pretty challenging," he said. "But it's something that's just so important to me, and I view it as very important to my culture and to many other people. To me it has broader implications."

Among those implications is what Williams feels is a disconnect between people and nature that is driving the controversies over sea otters. He believes that disconnect is what led to the initial overharvesting of sea otters two hundred years ago, which led to a further disconnect when otters were absent from the coastal environment for so many years.

American culture is very much disconnected right now from the environment and from our traditional ways of living for all of us," he said. "We're poisoning the earth because of that and exploiting it and each other because of that. When I talk about my work with sea otters, I'm really talking about culture and respect and spirituality and taking life and appreciating life."

Now that sea otters are back in a big way in Southeast Alaska, the vocal opposition to them from Natives and non-Natives alike is making Williams cringe. While he may be one of the few Native

Alaskans benefitting from the abundance of sea otters in the region, he is nostalgic about picking abalone and other traditional foods from the beach as a child. But he is also bothered by what he calls the "sea otter hate" that spews forth from too many people. The growing sea otter population in the region is directly attributable to the overexploitation of them centuries ago, he said, as was the unnatural abundance of shellfish and other marine invertebrates when sea otters were absent for so long.

"That imbalance is due to us, to human beings," he said. "So I'm hesitant to blame an animal for living, for thriving and expanding. That's life . . . and life is programmed to explore and expand. So I'm cautious about saying that's a problem because it seems like that's the natural order."

Chapter 10: Crash

ALEUTIAN ISLANDS, ALASKA

JIM ESTES had studied sea otters in the Aleutian Islands for nearly twenty years when he traveled once again to Amchitka Island in 1990. He went to see what he could learn about sea otter behavior in a population that was so large there was barely enough prey to sustain them. At the time, it was the only place in the world where sea otters had reached carrying capacity. When he arrived, he thought he knew most of what there was to know about the ecology of the resident otters that were thriving in the 1,200-mile arcing chain of islands in western Alaska. But things were about to change dramatically.

Sea otter numbers recovered rather quickly in the Aleutians after the end of the fur trade, but they did so in what Estes called "a spatially asynchronous manner." By that he meant that when legal sea otter hunting ended in 1911, the few otters that were left were found in tiny pockets scattered throughout the islands rather than evenly spread across the region. No one knows how many remained around Amchitka, but Estes described it as "just a handful, a very very few." There may have been one or two other sites in the Aleutians where otters survived, but even that is uncertain. Their recovery from such tiny numbers was initially quite slow, because the animals produce just one pup each year and perhaps because it was difficult to find mates when so few animals were left.

But when otter numbers finally started to build, they grew rapidly thanks to a healthy ecosystem with plenty of available prey.

Yet because sea otters are so dependent on the shallow coastal environment and females disperse only short distances, it took decades for the animals to spread from one island to the next. For example, when the otter population at Amchitka was completely recovered and filling almost every available corner of habitat, they had yet to make it to Shemya Island, just 225 miles to the west. By the late 1980s, however, most of their historic range across the Aleutian Islands had been recolonized; there were about six to seven thousand sea otters at Amchitka Island, and well over one hundred thousand in all of the Aleutians.

A number of surprises were awaiting Estes on his return to Amchitka, however. Up until then, everything had appeared to be happening as expected—the otters were keeping the sea urchins in check, and the kelp beds had recovered to support an abundance of fish and other marine life. His research plan for the next few years was to compare the behavior of the sea otters at Amchitka with those at Adak Island, 180 miles to the east, where the population was still recovering. He sought to compare parameters like growth rates and body conditions, birth and mortality rates, diets, time spent foraging, and other factors. He hoped to capture one hundred sea otters, place tracking devices on them, and study them in the same way he had conducted other research projects— by following each animal's activities from day to day.

The first surprise was how difficult it was to capture the animals. He expected to capture all one hundred sea otters in one week, but it took more than three weeks to capture just ninety. "At the time I reconciled it as just the way it was," Estes told me. "Maybe the weather was just too good and the animals were harder to capture for that reason. But that was the beginning of it all. Over the next two years as we studied those animals, every one of our hypotheses about what we expected in the sea otters of Amchitka Island just did not pan out."

Previously, when Estes began studying the Amchitka otters in the 1970s, it wasn't uncommon to find large numbers of dead otters as he walked the beaches. He collected data about the health, age, and gender of each one of them. Some days he found twenty or thirty otter carcasses, but he wasn't alarmed by them. When there are large numbers of animals in a population, it is expected that some will die and, in the case of sea otters, be washed onto the shore by the tides and waves. But during his two-year study of sea otters around Amchitka in 1990 and 1991, not one dead otter was found on any of the beaches.

"That was a huge surprise," he said. "I had no idea what was going on. All I knew was that I didn't know that ecosystem like I thought I did. I had gone out there expecting it was going to be a question of just documenting the things we already were fairly sure were true. Instead, I was really very humbled because I just didn't know what was happening."

When Estes followed up his Amchitka study with an analysis of sea otters at Adak Island—with similar results—he became convinced that sea otter populations in the region were declining rapidly. And the culprits, he believed, were killer whales.

THE 1995–1996 STUDY on Adak was primarily conducted by a young Tim Tinker working on his second sea otter research project. He and his wife, Julie, lived on Adak for a year, capturing and tracking sixty sea otters. During his time on the island, Tinker observed several killer whales attacking and eating sea otters. "I was sitting there on a cliff collecting foraging observations, and one of our tagged animals was really near shore, and all of a sudden she started periscoping. Something was going on," he said animatedly. "So I got my binoculars and I see these killer whale fins circling around this group of otters, and all of a sudden they came up and sucked down an otter. That was new to me. Then they ate a couple more and circled around and all of the otters fled. Most of the adult otters that had been offshore all suddenly were against the shore, craning their eyes and obviously very perturbed."

At the time, Tinker thought it was just an interesting natural-history observation. He didn't link the killer whale attacks to what he believed was a decline of the otter population around the island. When told about Tinker's hypothesis that otter numbers were slumping, Estes was skeptical until he returned to Adak and Tinker walked him through his reasoning. Estes found the explanation compelling. Still, he initially thought the decline was a local event rather than a region-wide population crash.

A key part of Tinker's evidence came from Clam Lagoon, a three-mile-long tidal pond with a sandbar across its mouth that prevents large marine mammals from entering. When the research project began, there were about one hundred sea otters living inside the lagoon and a similar number outside the lagoon. Four years later, 90 percent of the otters living outside the lagoon had dis-appeared, while numbers in the lagoon remained constant. Today there remains a healthy population of sea otters who spend nearly their entire lives inside Clam Lagoon, and none live outside it.

In 1997, Tinker and Estes surveyed several other islands in the Aleutians and found dramatic population declines everywhere they turned. They even conducted an underwater survey of the kelp beds around Adak Island and found massive numbers of sea urchins consuming the kelp, a sign that sea otters were virtually absent. An aerial survey of the entire Aleutian chain in 2000 turned up similar results. The scientists estimated that the Aleutian population of sea otters had sunk to less than 10 percent of its peak levels.

Their evidence of killer whale predation on sea otters included some unique otter behaviors that occur nowhere else. Tinker said that otters in the Aleutians now spend most of their time entirely hauled out of the water or resting on submerged rocks where the water is so shallow that killer whales can't reach them. "We've seen a complete behavioral shift across the entire Aleutians to avoid predators," he said. "It's so obvious what's going on out there when you see it."

But it was difficult for Tinker and Estes to convince their colleagues that killer whales were responsible for the sea otter decline. Their first research paper about it was rejected by a research journal. So they went back to work examining other possible explanations. Could the population decline be caused by contaminants from the military facilities on some of the Aleutian Islands? No, because sea otters experienced similar declines at pristine islands as well as those located near military bases. Was there a limitation on the availability of food? No, adult otters and their pups were observed to be robust and healthy, and as otter populations fell, more and more food was available. What about a disease? No dead otters were found washing up on coastal beaches, and when the researchers captured otters to test for diseases, they found no evidence of any illness. Which brought them back to the idea of predation by killer whales.

Little is known about the killer whales that live in the Aleutian Islands, because the area is difficult to get to and the animals are hard to study for any length of time. Like elsewhere in their range, there are two types of killer whales—transient animals (sometimes called Bigg's killer whales) that feed exclusively on marine mammals, and resident whales that eat only fish. According to Craig Matkin, a killer whale biologist with the North Gulf Oceanic Society in Homer, there are about 450 transient killer whales living in the Aleutian Islands and southern Bering Sea area, including the Pribilof Islands to the north of the Aleutian chain. In addition, Matkin claims there are several thousand resident killer whales that spend much of their time harassing the fishing fleet in the region. The mammal-eating transients are spread out thinly across the North Pacific, wandering back and forth in small groups across this massive body of water and feeding opportunistically on a mix of Steller sea lions, harbor seals, Dall's porpoises, northern fur seals, and juvenile whales, especially minke, gray, and humpback whales.

A sea otter, however, is a tiny piece of popcorn to a killer whale that typically consumes prey five or six times larger than the largest otter. To a killer whale, an otter is a little fur ball containing none of the precious blubber it prefers; it's barely a meal. And yet Tinker and Estes say that at least a few killer whales that traverse the Aleutian Islands somehow developed a taste for sea otters. In fact, all it would take is a few otter-eating killer whales to wipe out the region's entire sea otter population over a twenty-five-year period.

"The most plausible thing we came up with is that one matrilineal line of killer whales, just five or six related killer whales eating a few sea otters each per day, could be responsible for the entire Aleutian sea otter decline," said Tinker. "That's the mechanism that makes the most sense. And we watched it happen. We could see the same killer whales over and over again swimming through the kelp beds."

The development of novel behaviors among killer whales is not uncommon. Usually, the dominant female in a small group of whales may start to do something new—in this case, hunting and eating sea otters. That behavior then spreads to others in her pod through teaching and observation. "The idea that it started through cultural innovation among one group of killer whales is speculative," Tinker admits, but the idea "that killer whales are eating otters" is not.

Not everyone agrees.

Matkin is adamant that killer whales are not responsible for the dramatic decline in sea otter numbers in the Aleutians. He has observed killer whales killing sea otters in Kachemak Bay and Prince William Sound, but he says the otters usually aren't consumed. Instead, the whales use the otters as "training tools" to teach their offspring how to hunt and kill. And the numbers of otters killed are insignificant when compared to the total population.

"The only time I could imagine a killer whale taking sea otters as regular prey is if it was in a desperate situation," Matkin said. "Maybe it's lost most of its group and can't hunt like they usually do. . . . But switching to sea otters as their primary prey without a reason? That just doesn't make sense to me."

Estes and Tinker say there is a reason for the switch, though.

Prior to the sea otter population crash, the Aleutian population of Steller sea lions declined by about 80 percent in the 1970s and 1980s, and at least in the western Aleutians, the decline continues at about 4 to 6 percent annually. And the northern fur seal population has declined from about two million animals in the 1950s to about six hundred thousand today; though this was triggered initially by a culling of large numbers of females to protect commercial fisheries, the population continues to decline today for unknown reasons. Harbor seal numbers in the Aleutians are down about 80 percent, too, from their peak in the 1960s and no one can explain that, either.

This massive loss of marine mammal biomass in the Aleutian region over the last fifty years—all of which are species commonly eaten by killer whales—seems to Estes and Tinker like a logical reason for killer whales to go looking for new sources of food.

THE STELLER SEA LION population decline, which immediately preceded the beginning of the sea otter decline, seems to have been the last straw for the killer whales, at least if you believe Tinker and Estes. That apparently triggered the switch to a diet of sea otters, they say.

According to Doug Demaster, director of the Alaska Fisheries Science Center, which conducts extensive research on marine mammals in Alaska waters, Steller sea lions began declining rapidly in the 1980s. For most of that decade, 15 percent of the population died each year, which is a huge loss for any marine mammal population. Initially researchers speculated that the primary driver of the decline was fishermen, who could legally protect their catch by shooting any sea lion that was stealing their harvest or damaging their nets. Many fishermen also went to the sea lion rookeries and haul-out sites and illegally shot as many animals as they could find. When, in 1989, it finally became illegal to shoot Steller sea lions under any circumstances, the population decline eased to just 4 or 5 percent. The institution in 2001 of a fishing ban within a ten-mile buffer zone around sea lion rookeries in the eastern Aleutians put a halt to the decline, and the population there began to recover. But in the central and western Aleutians, the fishing industry claimed that a buffer would put them out of business, so they proposed instead to reduce their fishing effort by half. That doesn't seem to have worked, since Steller sea lion numbers continue to decline at about 5 percent per year in the region. No additional steps have been taken to reduce the decline, even though more than 450 sea lions were killed by human activities—mostly unintentional fishing-gear entanglement and hooking, though several were shot—between 2010 and 2014.

Demaster does not dispute the notion that killer whales are responsible for the dramatic decline of the sea otter population in the Aleutian Islands. But he's not convinced, as Estes and Tinker are, that the decline of Steller sea lions had anything to do with it. And he is even less convinced of the sea otter biologists' later hypothesis that explains the decline of the other marine mammals in the region.

According to Estes, killer whales started eating sea otters in the Aleutians right at the time that the Steller sea lions were at their lowest point, and the killer whales must have done so because there were so few sea lions around to eat. But as he thought about it more, he was led to another conclusion, one that became known as the sequential megafaunal collapse hypothesis. And it sparked significant controversy.

Estes looked back to the years prior to World War II when large whales were somewhat common in the North Pacific, before industrial-scale whaling caused a significant drop in whale numbers in the region. He said that those whales and their young were a key food resource for killer whales at the time. And when large numbers of whales were killed by commercial whalers in the 1950s and '60s, it caused a chain reaction that led killer whales to expand their diet and start feeding on smaller species. And one by one those smaller species declined as well—first fur seals, then Steller sea lions, and then harbor seals—until the killer whales got down to the smallest marine mammal of them all, the sea otter.

In the whale and marine mammal research community, this proposal didn't go over well. "There was a lot of emotion and a lot of pushback from those folks," Estes said. Tinker thinks that the individual pieces of the puzzle are less controversial than Estes's claim that all are connected and that one link in the chain caused the next. Everyone agrees, however, that there is little direct evidence to support the hypothesis. And yet there are so many unexplained population declines of marine mammals in the region that I found it almost comforting to have one theory explain them all. Tinker calls it "a great hypothesis that's hard to prove definitively."

One of the leading skeptics is Craig Matkin, who coauthored a scientific paper responding to Estes's ideas. He told me that there is no evidence suggesting that killer whales will approach a healthy population of animals and prey upon it until there are none left. He thinks other factors like environmental conditions, disease, or food availability caused the initial population declines, and killer whale predation may then be keeping the populations too low to recover. A shift in the Pacific Decadal Oscillation, a cycle of changing oceanographic conditions that warmed the North Pacific in the 1970s and may have caused many marine mammals to switch their preferred prey species, is one change many people suggest may have initiated the decline of seals and sea lions.

In light of the limited evidence for the sequential megafaunal collapse hypothesis, Demaster took the high road. "I don't think there is any argument that killer whales are an important factor in the dynamics of all the marine mammals in the Bering Sea and Gulf of Alaska and Aleutian Islands," he told me. "But I think the jury is still out in terms of how all these factors fit together. There are holes in all of the current hypotheses as to what explains the dynamics of these five marine mammal species over the last thirty years."

REGARDLESS OF WHAT caused the sea otter population in the Aleutians to crash—and who agrees or disagrees with that explanation—I wanted to see for myself what sea otters there were facing. I tried for two years to get on a research ship conducting periodic surveys of sea otters in portions of the island chain, but by the time each ship departed there were always too many scientists and not enough berths available to squeeze me in. So Renay and I trekked there on our own.

We flew into Unalaska Island, in the eastern third of the Aleutians, the most populous island in the chain and the one best known—at least recently—as the home base of the fishing vessels shown on the reality-television program *Deadliest Catch*. At first glance, Unalaska was nothing like I expected. I knew of its volcanic origins, but its steep, rocky slopes jutting up more than two thousand feet from the water's edge certainly made an unexpected impression as we arrived. Unlike Southeast Alaska and almost everywhere else I had visited in Alaska south of the Arctic Circle, the island was entirely treeless, save for a few spruces planted by soldiers during World War II. Instead, it was covered in lush grasses and wildflowers with scattered blueberry and salmonberry bushes. And though the island is the southernmost point in Alaska, closer in latitude to balmy Vancouver, British Columbia, than to the state's capital, many of the hillsides were still covered in snow on the first of July.

To cap it off, the island appeared to be relatively unaffected by the massive drop in sea otter numbers that the rest of the Aleutians have experienced. We noticed a few animals almost everywhere we turned. At least at first. A lone sea otter was in view from the airport terminal when we arrived from Anchorage, and as we ate our breakfast the next morning, we watched a grizzled male hard at work cracking open clams in a small inlet behind the island's only hotel. We saw a few other scattered individuals as well, but after a day of wandering around, our total was only six. Yet just a tiny corner of the 1,051-square-mile island is accessible to humans—the rest is roadless and uninhabited except by ptarmigans, lemmings, a few songbirds, and introduced Arctic ground squirrels and red foxes—so we figured there were plenty of other places the otters may reside.

About 4,300 people live on Unalaska and over a bridge to the tiny adjacent Amaknak Island, the largest human population anywhere in the Aleutians. Most work in or cater to the fishing, fish-processing, and marine-construction industries. Dutch Harbor, on Amaknak, is the nation's most productive fishing port, with 762 million pounds of pollock, salmon, king crab, and other species harvested in 2015 from the Bering Sea to the north and the Pacific Ocean to the south. Overlooking the harbor and scattered throughout the hillsides are moss-covered remnants of World War II fortifications and gun emplacements, evidence of the island's little-known military history as the only US site besides Pearl Harbor to be bombed by the Japanese.

After getting the lay of the land and taking a day to get used to the unusual daylight hours—sunrise at six thirty and sunset at midnight—Renay and I drove the length of every coastal road in the region to get a better sense of how the sea otter population was faring in the island's waters. We started at Unalaska Bay, across from our hotel, which was flat calm at dawn and absent of almost any wildlife save a small flock of harlequin ducks, several distant Dall's porpoises, and the ubiquitous pigeon guillemots, a mostly black seabird that was often the only bird species visible on the water. So we continued south along Captains Bay, where the noise from commercial fishing boats and seafood transport vessels was drowned out by the hum of fish processing plants; an absence of kelp in the bay suggested that otters weren't likely to be found in any numbers. We counted zero.

After a detour over and around Mount Newhall, we returned to the coast east of town at Summer Bay and Morris Cove, both absent of sea otters and almost any other wildlife. But as we rounded the corner toward Iliuliuk Bay, a fifty-foot-tall rocky spire called Little Priest Rock guarded a four-mile stretch of coastline where abundant kelp extended about one hundred yards offshore. Just beyond the spire we saw our first otter of the day, resting nearly motionless in the blustery cold. It made us feel optimistic about the upcoming shoreline, but that optimism didn't last long. Although we slowly scanned every piece of kelp and every bit of open water, we found no more otters. We were rewarded instead by several small groups of horned puffins, a couple Steller sea lions, more pigeon guillemots, and dozens of bald eagles. No otters were present in the tiny coves in town, either, even in the places we had seen individual animals the day before.

Our last chance was at the spit, a mile-long natural barrier that protects Dutch Harbor and the numerous ferries, Coast Guard vessels, research ships, and fishing boats docked there. It was a noisy place, as construction vehicles raced around twenty-five-foot-high stacks of crab pots covering every available spot of land. But on the outside edge of the spit, across Iliuliuk Bay from the stretch of kelp we had just driven by, another patch of kelp finally revealed what we had come nearly five thousand miles to see. A raft of about twenty sea otters groomed and rested just beyond the line of kelp, oblivious to our stares and even more oblivious to the abundant bald eagles—about eight hundred living in town at last count—that glared from every available perch.

A solitary male otter materialized not far from where we watched, uniform in color and with a healthy appearance suggesting he was approaching adulthood and happily in the prime of his life. He repeatedly dived on long foraging bouts, seldom resting between each dive, and never pausing to groom during the twenty minutes we observed him. When we first saw him surface, he carried a large cream-colored clam in both paws, then rolled on his back and began to noisily crack it open. We couldn't be sure what kind of tool he was using to crush the hard shell—it appeared to be a flat stone—but his effort resulted in a great deal of splashing, as if it were a child's pool party. With his face turned to the side to avoid the splashing, he quickly struck the clam on the stone four or five times, paused momentarily, then repeated the process until the shell was broken enough that he could remove the flesh with his teeth. He dropped the empty shell into the water and hurriedly followed it down in search of his next course. When he reappeared, he brought up an unidentifiable white fleshy mass—perhaps a squid or sea squirt—that the otter repeatedly tugged at with both paws in an unsuccessful attempt to tear it apart. His flat rock was of no use this time. He bit it a few times, but soon appeared to decide it wasn't worth the effort, so he dropped it and dived for something else.

As eight other solo otters foraged in peace amid the thick kelp and a harbor seal looked on from a distance, the animal continued his foraging dives, always surfacing with something edible that required additional effort before he could swallow it. Foraging for food was hard work requiring his full attention, and never once was he distracted from his effort by the commotion of other otters or by the rumble of fishing boats docked just one hundred yards away in the harbor. The few times he glanced up occurred as he was chewing his food prior to diving again. He looked to be saying to himself that there was no time to waste, and given how much food each otter requires every day, he was probably right.

I closed my eyes for a moment to concentrate on the sound of the sea otters smashing open their mollusks, though it was some-times difficult to pinpoint the direction from which the rhythmic rat-a-tat-tats came. While I focused my ears on the sea otter drum-beat, one otter provided a new musical voice by sneezing in the distance. And as I opened my eyes and scanned the deeper water, I kept finding more and more otters, many of which were also for-aging and loudly cracking mollusks. One brought up a large crab and silently broke its legs off before digging into the crab's innards.

My tally neared forty when the original raft of sea otters appeared to wake up at once and roll around momentarily before returning to rest. They drifted farther from shore, farther from the kelp, then seemed to split into smaller groups before recombining again. A smaller raft I hadn't seen before paddled to join the party, and a few brief spats erupted before everyone settled once more. And still the staccato tapping continued, like the sound of woodpeckers drilling into a dead tree.

The seemingly healthy number of sea otters at the Dutch Harbor spit belied the true nature of the complicated Aleutian otter story, as we learned the next day. Our visit to Unalaska coincided with the conclusion of a research expedition throughout the east-ern Aleutians by scientists studying kelp, urchins, and the changing ecosystem brought about by the drastic reduction in sea otter numbers. Based aboard the RV *Oceanus*, a 177-foot oceanographic research vessel, a team of thirteen scientists and graduate students dived to the seafloor near Atka, Adak, Tanaga, Chuginadak, Umnak, Anagula, and Unalaska Islands to assess urchin numbers, kelp health, and the diversity of other marine life in the region following the sea otter decline. While they didn't conduct a scientific census of sea otters, they were surprised to observe an average of just one otter per island, with the exception of Unalaska.

"They're really scarce out there," said Ben Weitzman, who works for Tim Tinker and is studying for his doctorate at the University of Alaska. "They don't make themselves very conspicuous. When you observe them, it's always very near shore, you don't find large rafts anywhere, and they don't hang out very far from where they can get to shore to haul out" in case a killer whale appears.

Weitzman had participated in systematic surveys of the Aleutians the previous two years, circumnavigating each island and counting every otter found, and he said that counts were very low, especially around the western islands. Sea otter numbers hadn't declined much from previous surveys, but because there are so few otters left, many island populations are at great risk of simply disappearing entirely.

WESTWARD OF THE Aleutian Islands, across the international date line to Russia's Commander Islands and southward to the Kuril Islands, some of the same questions are being asked about the resident sea otter populations. And yet the situation there is so very different. Though separated from the Aleutians by just 207 miles, the two islands that make up the Commander Islands have a stable sea otter population numbering about seven thousand animals (though they are infrequently surveyed).

"It basically looks exactly like the Aleutians but before the decline," said Tinker. "You have scrawny otters that are pretty much limited by food abundance. There are killer whales there, but there's no indication that they're eating sea otters. The otters rest offshore in groups, oblivious to the killer whales, just like they used to do in the Aleutians."

The Kuril Island sea otters, however, have experienced a rapid decline in the last decade just like those in the Aleutians, although for apparently different reasons. Otter numbers in the eight-hundred-mile island chain that runs southwest from the Kamchatka Peninsula almost to Japan totaled about twenty-two thousand in the early 2000s, with more than half of that total observed around just one of the archipelago's fifty-six islands, Shumshu Island in the north. But five years later, the population had declined by 70 percent for unknown reasons.

According to Russian sea otter biologist Katya Ovsyanikova, who conducted an otter survey throughout the Kurils in 2012, the population decline is not likely caused by killer whales, since most of the killer whales observed in the region are residents that eat only fish, and sea otters there have not changed their behavior to avoid killer whales. She told me that pollution and human disturbance appear to be the greatest threats; while some poaching occurs, there is no market anywhere for sea otter pelts, so hunting is unlikely to be a significant concern.

Ovsyanikova said she is particularly worried about the sea otter population at Urup Island, where she found about 850 otters during her latest survey, the second-largest population in the Kurils but less than half the number counted a decade earlier. She said the island has long been recognized for its importance to sea otters, and it was a protected nature reserve from 1958 to 2003. Despite plans to reestablish its protected status by 2018, a gold-mining operation opened there in 2013, and explosives and liquid cyanide are used to extract the gold. Ovsyanikova said the significant disturbance is placing the sea otter population at great risk, and she argues that the island should be recognized as critical habitat.

The farther south one goes in the Kuril Islands, the fewer sea otters are found. And though northern Japan had a small historic population of otters before the fur trade, sea otters no longer inhabit the region, except for a very occasional stray animal that will wander south of the Kurils to Japan's Hokkaido Island.

"There's been a couple of times that individual males have shown up there for a couple weeks, and once they had a population of two males for a month or so," Tinker said. "But it's at the range edge there, and what may be limiting them there, no one knows."

MY VISIT TO UNALASKA ISLAND and observation of fewer than fifty sea otters clearly didn't do much to answer the larger questions about the decline of sea otters and other marine mammals in the Aleutian Islands. But it made me ponder what may be the most pressing question for the region's sea otters: What's next? Has the population decline ended? What is the outlook for their recovery? And what can be done to accelerate that recovery?

The answers to those questions are just as complicated as the explanations for the population's decline. Most experts seem to think that it has ended, but they also see little evidence that sea otters in the Aleutians are recovering. "There are so few otters out there that it's hard to say what the trends are," Estes said. "I think for the last decade the population has been more or less stable at a very low density." He noted that there are a few places where the animals have become locally extinct, like on isolated Buldir Island in the far western Aleutians, which Estes said had about one thousand sea otters at its peak but now has none. Most islands still have a few sea otters in locations where there is habitat inaccessible to killer whales, like at Clam Lagoon and around Eddy Island. In those locations, the otters are producing pups at a relatively high rate, but they're still not growing the population.

Why not? Estes and Tinker say it's because killer whales still occasionally visit the islands and eat a few sea otters. "During the heyday of the decline in the early 1990s when the population really declined rapidly," Estes said, "we saw killer whales around all the time. Every day we would see them. But now I might see a killer whale every couple of years. So I think what's happened is that they came, they ate the otters, and they left, and now occasionally one will come back, and any otter that's not smart enough to get out of a place that's vulnerable will probably get eaten."

Doug Demaster agrees. He calls it "the predator pit," when populations get so small that even a low level of mortality caused by predation can prevent the population from recovering. He thinks that's what is happening with Steller sea lions in the western Aleutians and also what is happening with sea otters. "They're going to have to survive in such low numbers that the killer whales move off or lose their cultural memory of feeding on sea otters," he said. "My guess is that there will be local areas where the otter numbers were knocked down so far that just a few killer whales predating on them would prevent recovery. And there will be other areas where killer whales for some reason stop foraging on otters or somehow aren't finding the otters and they'll start recovering in those areas. So over the next twenty years, some areas will have no recovery and other areas will have reasonable recovery."

Sadly, there is little that can be done to help the sea otters recover more quickly. All of the animals involved—seals and sea lions, killer whales and sea otters—are protected by the Marine Mammal Protection Act. Some, like the sea otters and Steller sea lions, have dual protection under the Endangered Species Act. So it is very difficult to take steps to help one species without harming one of the others. Demaster says it may be possible to implement a program to harass the killer whales using underwater acoustics to keep them out of certain small areas, to allow the otters to recover. But there is no telling whether that would be successful over the long term. Federal biologists have tried such an effort only a few times, mostly to scare California sea lions away from the mouths of salmon-spawning rivers in Washington and Oregon, and it didn't work especially well. Attempting it in a large, remote place like the Aleutian Islands would be even more challenging, not to mention extremely expensive. It would also be highly controversial—killer whales may have as many supporters among the general public as sea otters do—and likely take a long time to be approved.

Estes has another idea. Given his belief that the otter decline was part of a cascade of effects that started with the decline of the great whales, he thinks the recovery of these whales would trigger a reverse cascade that would lead to the recovery of the Aleutian sea otters. "It's not absolutely clear that it will run in reverse," he said, "but I think that if someone were to ask me what's the most likely way of fixing this problem, I'd say recover the whales."

If that's really the answer, then that could be considered good news, because whale populations are recovering throughout the Pacific. Humpback whale numbers are growing, gray whales are on the increase, minke whale numbers are high, and fin and sperm whale numbers are uncertain but probably stable. But getting the next domino in the cascade to right itself may take a while, and sea otters may recover on their own in that time, regardless of what happens to the rest of the marine mammals in the region.

Chapter 11: Translocation

OLYMPIC PENINSULA, WASHINGTON

AMCHITKA ISLAND doesn't play a role in just the discovery of the sea otter population crash in the Aleutian Islands. The story of Amchitka's sea otters is much bigger than that. Located just nine hundred miles across the icy Bering Sea from Russia's Kamchatka Peninsula, this narrow forty-two-mile-long island has had no permanent human population since the 1830s. But its population of wildlife includes more than one hundred species of migratory birds, rare nesting seabirds, and thousands of marine mammals like walruses and Steller sea lions. Its natural wonders were so extraordinary that in 1913, President William Howard Taft designated the island the centerpiece of what is now the Alaska Maritime National Wildlife Refuge. But the island has been repurposed several times since then. During World War II, its fragile tundra landscape became an airfield for thousands of US soldiers fighting the Aleutian Islands campaign. When they departed, they left behind tons of debris and little surviving wildlife. The island was then turned back over to the US Fish and Wildlife Service, which undertook a different kind of campaign, one that restored to health the formerly abundant wildlife. Salmon returned to spawn in its streams, bald eagles and Aleutian cackling geese were plentiful, and sea otter numbers skyrocketed.

By the early 1960s, however, things were about to change again, dramatically. That's when the Department of Defense and the Atomic Energy Commission went looking for a site to conduct underground tests of nuclear bombs. Despite strong objections, especially concerns that it would trigger an earthquake and tsunami, an eighty-kiloton bomb called Long Shot was exploded there belowground in 1965, followed by the one-megaton Milrow in 1969. Descriptions of the latter blast noted that it "forced geysers of mud and water from local streams and lakes fifty feet into the air" and "turned the surrounding sea to froth." More objections were raised when the commission announced that an even larger nuclear device, the five-megaton Cannikin, would be detonated a mile below the surface of Amchitka in 1971, the largest underground nuclear test in US history and nearly four hundred times larger than the bomb that destroyed Hiroshima.

Among those objecting were US Fish and Wildlife Service biologists and others from the Alaska Department of Fish and Game. They argued that the recently restored wildlife populations would be wiped out—they were—and that the government should take steps to mitigate those effects. Noting the many C-130 cargo planes delivering supplies to the island and departing empty, the biologists proposed using the aircraft to deliver Amchitka sea otters to parts of their range where the animals had yet to become reestablished following the fur trade, such as Washington and Oregon. Seeking some positive publicity after years of negative coverage, the Atomic Energy Commission agreed to the idea and even agreed to fund most of it. But transporting the otters wasn't easy.

Long before Jim Estes made his first appearance on Amchitka, biologist Karl Kenyon had been studying sea otters there, often experimenting with methods of capturing and holding the animals for the purpose of relocating them elsewhere, a process biologists call translocation. Experimental translocations had been conducted six times between 1951 and 1959. Kenyon tried keeping sea otters in dry bedding, in freshwater, and in various saltwater enclosures, but in all but the last scenario, the animals died because during the time between capture and release, their fur became matted and soiled, and the otters were unable to groom themselves effectively. It was not well understood at that time how important a well-groomed pelage was to the well-being of sea otters. When the captive otters were released back into the cold Pacific, they quickly became hypothermic and died.

By 1968, however, sea otters had been successfully reintroduced to Southeast Alaska and to the tiny island of Saint Paul in the Pribilof Islands, north of the Aleutian chain. Not all of them survived the process, but Kenyon and his colleagues considered it somewhat successful and worth continuing, especially since it was likely that most of the otters around Amchitka would die as a result of the detonation of Cannikin. So they decided that Washington and Oregon would be the next destination for translocated sea otters.

On Amchitka in 1969, the biologists captured twenty-nine sea otters destined for Point Grenville, Washington, on the wild coast of the Olympic Peninsula. They captured the animals using a fishermen's gill net, loaded the otters into specially designed crates, and hauled them to the Amchitka airfield, where they were stowed aboard a C-130 and flown to a small airport near the release site. From the airport, the otters were trucked to the coast and, before a crowd of reporters and onlookers, unceremoniously released on the beach. Karl Schneider, a retired biologist with the Alaska Department of Fish and Game, was there, and in a 2014 story in *Audubon* magazine, he explained how cages of frantic, filthy sea otters were opened on the beach in a circus-like atmosphere. Some were even prodded with poles to leave their cages and enter the water. Two weeks later, sixteen of the animals had already washed ashore dead (two from gunshot wounds). None of the twenty-nine are believed to have survived.

Kenyon and his colleagues tried again a year later, this time releasing thirty sea otters at Cake Island, north of the community of La Push, which borders Olympic National Park, and those animals fared better. No immediate mortality was reported. By then the biologists had learned that the otters should not just be pushed into the water after their long trip from Amchitka. Instead, Kenyon and his colleagues designed and constructed large holding pens that could be anchored in the water offshore so the animals could acclimatize to their new environment for several days. The twenty-four-foot-square pens had a shelf around the edge where the otters could haul out to rest and groom, a fence around the perimeter, and a fine-mesh net at the bottom prohibiting them from escaping to the open ocean too soon.

That strategy was attempted in Oregon that same year. Again, Karl Kenyon captured twenty-nine sea otters on Amchitka and they were transported via C-130 aircraft, this time to an old military base near the release site of Port Orford, sixty miles north of the California border. The otters made it successfully into the holding pens, where they were held for two days, and the animals appeared to quickly acclimatize to their new environment. The pens were then towed by a fishing boat three miles south to Redfish Rocks—now a marine reserve—where it was believed the habitat would support the animals.

Ron Jameson was a senior at Oregon State University in 1970, when the first sea otters were translocated to the state, and he wrote a school paper about the project. He later spent thirty years study-ing otters in the Pacific Northwest for the US Fish and Wildlife Service. As a result, he knows more than anyone alive today about the circumstances of the Oregon otter translocations, and he said it wasn't pretty.

"It was really nasty weather when they towed the pens, and the trip was quite harrowing for the otters," Jameson said. "When they got there, some of them didn't even want to leave the pens." But the nets were cut anyway, the animals were released, and by the time the boat returned to Port Orford, most of the otters had already arrived back in port ahead of the boat. The animals appar-ently wanted no part of Redfish Rocks. No one bothered to keep track of the otters after that, so little is known of their ultimate fate.

A year later, in June 1971, another twenty-four sea otters were destined for release at Port Orford, and forty more were translo-cated fifty miles farther north to South Cove at Cape Arago, near the town of Coos Bay. And once again, the weather wreaked havoc on the biologists' plans. A storm blew in rough seas and howling winds, making it nearly impossible to safely release the animals into the pens. Jameson doesn't believe that any of the otters at either site made it as far as the pens but were instead just dumped overboard from their crates. No one made any effort to monitor the status of those animals, either.

After he graduated, Jameson returned to Oregon State University to earn a master's degree studying the state's otter pop-ulation, but what he found was not promising. In 1973 he located a total of twenty-three sea otters, eighteen of which were congre-gated at Blanco Reef, a group of rocks fourteen miles north of Port Orford that is now part of the Oregon Islands National Wildlife Refuge. One otter had wandered 160 miles north to Gull Rock, near the appropriately named village of Otter Rock; two more were found near Port Orford; and the last two were at Simpson Reef near Cape Arago. Three years later, just twelve sea otters were observed in the entire state of Oregon, all at Blanco Reef, and by 1981, when just one animal was left, the population was all but extirpated and the translocation effort deemed a failure. The only good news was that the Oregon otters successfully produced ten pups, but where they ended up is unknown.

Jameson thinks he knows what happened to many of the released animals. "My personal hypothesis is that ultimately they started trickling out and moving north," he said. "I would almost bet money that some of the first otters that turned up at Destruction Island in Washington, which was nowhere near where the Washington otters were released, could very well have come from Oregon. After some period of time, I think they just started to disperse, and I suspect that a lot of them headed for home"—toward Alaska.

It's a fair hypothesis, but there is no evidence to back it up. At the time, the tracking devices commonly used today by biologists to monitor hundreds of species around the globe, like GPS-based satellite tracking systems, had not yet been developed. The translocated sea otters weren't even identified with flipper tags or any other device to indicate they were part of a special population released at a certain site. When young Jameson called a biologist in Washington to see what he knew about the otters that had been released there, he was told that no one knew anything about them, and if they disappeared, the biologists would just go get some more from Alaska. The passage of the Marine Mammal Protection Act, however, made that prospect much more difficult. With the exception of the experimental group brought to San Nicolas Island in California as part of the establishment of the state's no-otter zone, wild sea otters would never again be translocated anywhere in North America.

Yet despite the absence of a resident population, sea otters have a strong fan base in Oregon. Quinn Read, the wildlife coordinator for the nonprofit advocacy group Oregon Wild, said "there is a public appetite for sea otter recovery" in the state, though she laments the fact that it does not appear to be on the radar of the state Department of Fish and Wildlife. "They're listed as threatened in the state, and yet they do not appear on the wildlife agency's website," she told a gathering of sea otter biologists in Seattle in 2015. "So I think that speaks to where we're at in Oregon." Her organization is pushing for state officials to develop a sea otter recovery plan that identifies potential habitat, determines how to address human conflicts, and develops a plan for restoring the population.

Read has every reason to feel optimistic. Even if the state does nothing, most observers agree that sea otters will soon begin to naturally reestablish a population in the state. Since 2008, more than twenty-five individual sea otters have found their way to Oregon. Most have been seen along the northern part of the coastline near Newport, close to where the last known Oregon otter was killed in the fur trade in 1907. Jameson calls the visiting animals "stragglers and dispersers from the Washington population." Some have been found dead on beaches, and all that have been identified have been males. "The thing that will really determine whether we're going to reestablish a population is if we get a young female or two that decide to wander off down here," Jameson said. "I think one of these days we're going to get some females with pups in Washington that move quite a bit farther south, and eventually they're going to wander into Oregon. It may take a while, and it's possible that we may get some wandering up from California, too, but it's going to happen."

UNLIKE IN OREGON, the translocated population of sea otters in Washington eventually flourished, but regular monitoring of the Washington animals didn't begin until 1977, seven years after their release. By then, the population had declined to just nineteen individuals, four of which were pups. A year later there were just twelve, and no pups. But then their numbers began growing—to forty-five in 1981 and ninety-nine in 1988, before doubling a year later. Over the next twenty years, sea otter numbers in Washington grew at a rate nearing 10 percent per year. All of the animals were found along the outer coast of the Olympic Peninsula, well north of the original translocation sites.

So that's where I headed. I arrived on the peninsula at Port Angeles on the Strait of Juan de Fuca and proceeded west toward the outer coast. But along the way I decided to conduct an informal survey of sea otters in the strait. Heading west on State Route 112, which hugged the coastline almost all the way, I pulled over every chance I could to scan the water with my binoculars. I wasn't expecting much, because the official surveys had found few otters in the strait in recent years. But that didn't stop me from trying. Back in the mid-1990s, more than 120 sea otters, almost all males, rounded the corner into the strait, where they hung out in some of the westernmost bays during the winter months and ate all the available red sea urchins in a span of five or six years before retreating back to the outer coast. Yet I figured there were bound to be a few lingering where I could see them.

But there weren't. I found not one sea otter foraging in the abundant bull kelp near the tiny fishing village of Sekiu, none at beautiful Neah Bay, not even any at Cape Flattery, the northwesternmost point of the Lower 48, where seabirds, porpoises, and sea lions were abundant. And yet, apparently, the results of my highly unscientific assessment were wrong, though not by much. The week before my informal survey, officials with the Washington Department of Fish and Wildlife, the US Fish and Wildlife Service, the Seattle Aquarium, and other agencies conducted their own sea otter survey of the state's coastline using airplanes and land-based spotters, and they found a total of 1,394 sea otters in the state, including one in the Strait of Juan de Fuca. I don't feel bad about missing that one animal in the vast strait.

According to Steve Jeffries, the biologist who coordinates sea otter surveys for the Washington Department of Fish and Wildlife, the sea otter population in the state has been growing at a rate of about 5 to 7 percent in recent years. Strangely, the distribution pattern of the population has flip-flopped, with about 70 percent of the animals now in the southern portion of their range—roughly between the town of La Push and Willoughby Rock in the Copalis National Wildlife Refuge, a distance of about 60 miles—whereas the northern section of the range had previously been home to the majority of Washington sea otters prior to about 2000. It appears that the northern region may have reached its sea otter carrying capacity, while there is still abundant food and habitat for the animals to continue expanding to the south.

The greatest numbers of sea otters counted in the 2015 survey were found at Destruction Island, a thirty-acre island located more than three miles off the coast just north of the Quinault tribal reservation, which borders Olympic National Park. Part of the Quillayute Needles National Wildlife Refuge, Destruction Island looks, from an unmarked roadside overlook, like a low, flat mound of rock and earth covered in abundant green vegetation. It is topped by a prominent black-and-white lighthouse and at least two unidentifiable man-made structures. The island was too far away for me to see any sea otters, but I knew they were there. Hundreds of them. In fact, according to the survey, there were 386 sea otters living in the waters around the island about the time I was there, and a year later 687 otters were seen in one massive raft a short distance north.

Destruction is the largest island on Washington's outer coast, and Jeffries says it is usually home to more than half of the state's sea otters because it provides everything a healthy otter needs. "It has many fingers of protected areas where the otters can raft up; it has a lot of lee areas so when the wind is blowing they can hang out protected from the wind," he said. "And it's right in the middle of pretty good, if not the best, Dungeness crab habitat on the Washington coast." The otters radiate out from Destruction Island to forage, eating as many crabs as they can find. The crabs in the areas that are too deep for the otters to reach will continually repopulate the otter foraging area. From a sea otter's perspective, it's the ideal place to live, though the tribal crab fishermen who fish in the area would prefer that the otters moved elsewhere.

Although a few scattered individual sea otters occasionally wander south of Destruction Island, it seemed odd to me that there have been no mass movements of otters attempting to recol-onize the southern two-thirds of the Washington coast. Jeffries thinks the reason has mostly to do with the distribution of the two species of kelp found in the area. Giant kelp is a perennial seaweed that can grow a foot or two each day and can easily reach more than one hundred feet tall. It has willowy, leaflike fronds and gas-filled bladders that hold it upright in the water. The closely related bull kelp, on the other hand, is an annual seaweed, which means it breaks off and dies back every year before growing back again. Jeffries said that Washington sea otters are primarily found where giant kelp grows year-round, and there is almost no giant kelp in the state south of Destruction Island, just bull kelp. In the winter, when the wind and water conditions are at their roughest, sea otters raft together in large groups in the protection of the kelp, where they can anchor themselves and stick together. Since the only patches of kelp available in winter are of the giant variety, that's where the otters tend to spend most of their time, and this keeps them from expanding southward.

Because the entire Washington population of sea otters is confined to a one-hundred-mile stretch of coastline, Jeffries says the greatest threat to the state's otters is an oil spill. Unlike in California and Alaska, diseases have not been a serious problem for the otter population in Washington. They aren't facing significant predation from sharks or killer whales, either, thanks to an abundant population of harbor seals. "Why would a predator choose to eat a fur ball like an otter when it can eat a little cube of butter?" Jeffries asked. But an oil spill would be a major disaster for Washington's otters. The last time an oil spill struck Washington's coast was just three months before the massive Exxon Valdez spill in Alaska, when a fuel barge, the *Nestucca*, spilled 231,000 gallons of fuel oil at the entrance to Grays Harbor. The oil spread south to Newport, Oregon, and north to Vancouver Island. If that happened today, the Washington sea otter population may not be able to recover.

ONE OF THE OFFICIAL participants in the annual Washington sea otter surveys was Jessie Hale, a graduate student at the University of Washington, where she studies sea otters under the guidance of professor Kristin Laidre. Hale invited me to join her research team for a couple days to learn how the diet of sea otters in the region has changed in the forty years since the animals were first translocated to the state. I met her and undergraduate research technician Abby Van Hemmen at the Ozette Lake campground in Olympic National Park, and we drove for twenty minutes along restricted-access logging roads through patches of old-growth spruce and fir forest and small, recent clear-cuts highlighted by generous stalks of foxglove. At the end of the road, three cabins and a trailer were hidden in the trees at the edge of a cliff known as Duk Point, one of five sites Hale uses to observe sea otter foraging behavior. A tiny observation point was carved from the salal shrubs at the edge of the cliff, a spot just large enough for the three of us to stand. From our vantage point, we could see a group of a dozen exposed boulders lying three hundred yards offshore, most no larger than a Volkswagen Beetle. A couple miles to the south we could see Bodelteh Islands, sea stacks considered the westernmost point of land in the Lower 48.

Hale quickly scanned the nearby waters with her high-powered telescope and counted twelve sea otters within easy view, and she immediately homed in on the one individual located closest to shore. Without a word of explanation, she began to call out data. Van Hemmen had already pulled out a stopwatch and clipboard filled with prepared data sheets, and she started writing. It was 4:14 p.m. when Van Hemmen started the stopwatch at the moment Hale called out "down" to indicate the otter had started its foraging dive. Thirty-three seconds later, when Hale called "up," Van Hemmen clicked the stopwatch again and made some notes on her clipboard. Wearing a black eye patch to combat eye strain during long hours of staring through her telescope, Hale mumbled to herself as she tried to identify the variety of prey with which the animal returned to the surface. "Well, whatever it is," she finally said, "it's really enjoying it." Although identifying prey is the focus of Hale's research, it isn't easy. It is not uncommon for her to be unsure of what is being eaten. Frankly, I was amazed that she could ever identify from two hundred yards whether it was a snail or crab or clam, let alone the particular species involved. I tried repeatedly and failed every time. All I could see was a tiny blur being quickly manipulated in the otter's paws. I seldom could even tell what color the prey was, let alone its shape or size, before the animal finished eating it and submerged again.

"Down," Hale called out once more, and less than a minute later, "up." She tries to observe twenty-five consecutive foraging dives from one otter before moving on to the next animal. Any more than that and she says it may skew her results. But she often struggles to reach twenty-five. The otters sometimes move out of view or stop foraging entirely and begin to groom, or a male may arrive and attempt to mate with the target female. And other otters will sometimes join the foraging activity, which often results in Hale's losing track of which animal she is focused on as they repeatedly dive and surface together.

At 4:49, she moved on to another otter, one that was located farther north and out of the sun. She provided a running narration for the next twelve minutes of everything the otter did, from diving and surfacing to smacking the prey on its chest and rolling around in the water. At 5:02, a young male otter cruised in close to shore, grooming, vocalizing, and looking around, followed minutes later by a female, which turned out to be its mother. Hale focused her telescope on the pair and had a much easier time identifying prey items. The first one was a crab, which the mother shared with her pup. On her next dive, the female otter surfaced with another crab, which she ate almost entirely herself, sharing only one leg with the pup. After momentarily swimming out of sight, she surfaced with a large ochre sea star, which she bit twice and dropped. "She definitely didn't like the taste of that," Hale said with a smirk. Two dives later the otter surfaced with several small items, probably snails, then did so again. But after eight dives, both otters disappeared behind some trees. And given the continuously poor lighting conditions and the distance that most otters were from our observation point—not to mention our own hunger—Hale announced we were calling it a day.

IN THE 1990s, biologists established twenty-nine sea otter observation points along the Olympic Peninsula from which to study and monitor otters that were tagged during earlier research projects. Some of those sites were also used to collect data about sea otter foraging from 1993 to 1999 and again in 2011 and 2012. So Hale used those same sites for her foraging studies, enabling her to compare how otter prey in those locations may have changed through the years. She began her study in 2014 and planned to continue making monthly observations at her five sites until at least 2017.

Scientists speculate that the otters are probably consuming smaller prey than they did in the 1990s because the larger prey have already been eaten by earlier generations of sea otters. "The assumption is that when sea otters move into an area, it's kind of pristine and it's got this really huge invertebrate population with gigantic urchins. And then the otters come in and eat their favorite food first, which in Washington is usually urchins," Hale explained. "Then they work their way down the food web, kind of like a buffet, starting with their favorite things and moving to their second-favorite things. The assumption is that by now they've eaten all of their favorite foods and are now eating smaller stuff."

Hale has already found that hypothesis to be somewhat true. Based on her preliminary data, the otters are eating a great many more snails than they did in the 1990s, while consuming fewer urchins and clams. The majority of their diet in the '90s was clams, but clams became the second most common prey a decade later. At the southern end of their Washington range, near the resort area of Kalaloch, where otters have only recently been observed and where they have not yet consumed all of their preferred prey, Hale observed the animals eating Dungeness crabs and razor clams.

After we discussed Hale's sea otter research at our campsite late into the night, I was awakened in my tent the next morning by the loud croaking of a pair of ravens. When I went looking for them at a walkway over an outlet stream of Ozette Lake, I found five river otters careening about in the water—a mother and pup on one side of the bridge and three more pups romping about together on the other side. The ravens were perched on a downed log by the river's edge right next to the group of three pups, and the birds' noisy vocalizations suggested to me that they were hoping the otters were going to catch some fish that the ravens would confiscate for their breakfast.

River otters are the only other species of otter in North America, and they are quite easy to distinguish from sea otters. River otters are primarily found in freshwater, though they are occasionally found in quiet saltwater bays, and they are less than half the size of sea otters. They also spend half of their time out of the water, have small paws that enable them to be adept at running on land, and they swim on their bellies, all of which are vastly different from sea otter behaviors. In addition, river otters give birth to as many as four pups at once, compared to the single pup of a sea otter, and river otters are almost always found alone or in small family groups, never in large rafts. And while on first glance the two species may appear similar, I find that sea otters tend to have a shaggy look compared to the well-coiffed, sleek river otters.

Among the thirteen species of otter on earth, just one other species besides the sea otter—the rare and little-known marine otter of coastal Chile, Peru, and extreme southern Argentina—confines itself to salt water rather than fresh. But it tops out at just twelve pounds and spends most of its time on land, so it is unlikely to be mistaken for a sea otter.

HALE AND VAN HEMMEN were awake when I returned to our campsite after watching the river otters, and we soon departed for Duk Point again. When we arrived, the lighting was good and several otters were foraging somewhat close by. Hale homed in on one animal whose first dive resulted in a crab—Dungeness or kelp crab, most likely, though several other varieties were possible, too. The female otter brought up a mass of seaweed encased with snails in its next three dives before a male arrived and attempted to mate. "Ooh, ow, that hurts," Hale cried out anxiously as she watched. "He's really biting her. Yikes!" And as fast as the mating attempt started, it was over. The male moved on, and the female returned to foraging. It brought up more seaweed, then two or three snails at a time, and once I even noticed it removing a snail from the pouch in its armpit. During a thirty-eight-minute period, the otter made the requisite twenty-five foraging dives, the first time Hale had recorded the target number of dives since I arrived.

As we waited for another sea otter to begin foraging, Hale pointed out several animals exhibiting what she considered typical—and entertaining—behaviors. She called one "touch-down hands," when the otter raised both paws vertically in the air, probably to keep them warm and dry, which made it look like the animal was a referee signaling a touchdown. Another behavior she called "Hula-Hooping" involved an otter raising all four append-ages in the air while simultaneously rolling in the water. And just prior to departing Duk Point for the morning, Hale laughed as she observed an otter rub its belly with one paw and pat its head with the other, a skill I never successfully accomplished as a child and one that I decided not to attempt while Hale and Van Hemmen were watching. "They often do two different behaviors with their hands at the same time," she said, "but more often they scratch their head with one paw and scratch their armpit with the other." I couldn't help but laugh at the image that brought to mind.

The next otter Hale studied repeatedly brought to the surface much larger prey than did the previous otters we had observed, though she also came up empty handed more often. On her first dive she captured a gumboot chiton, a massive gastropod that Hale first thought was a sea cucumber. Van Hemmen noted on her data sheet that the chiton was "a three-plus," meaning it was more than three times the size of the sea otter's paw. The otter quickly ate half of it before diving again. That time she captured nothing. The next time she surfaced with a large red sea urchin, another prey item judged to be a three-plus. After another unsuc-cessful dive, she retrieved a slightly smaller red urchin followed by a midsize purple urchin, nothing, three mussels, and another red urchin.

As we departed Duk Point, I asked Hale why the last two otters we observed had captured such different prey items even though they were foraging quite close to each other. Why didn't the first otter find the same large prey that the second one found? Were they simply specialists in different kinds of prey? I would have guessed that both would have captured whatever opportunistic prey items they stumbled upon and would have had an equal likelihood of finding a large urchin or chiton. With a quick glance at the data sheet, Hale came up with a plausible answer. She said the first otter made very short dives but succeeded in capturing something every time. It probably settled for lesser-quality prey so it could return to the surface more quickly. The second otter stayed below the surface for longer periods than the first animal and was unsuccessful at capturing any prey almost half the time. But when it captured something, it was usually pretty big. Was there a physical reason that restricted the first animal to shorter dives? Hale didn't think so. She guessed that they were simply two different foraging strategies, perhaps learned from previous generations. "Someone should attempt a cost-benefit analysis of the two foraging strategies," said Hale. "But it's not going to be me."

Chapter 12: Walter

THE CALL FROM Tofino, British Columbia, came in to the Marine Mammal Rescue Center at the Vancouver Aquarium just after dinnertime on October 17, 2013. Someone had reported to the local police that a sea otter in the harbor had an injured flipper and was unusually lethargic. The animal had been hanging around in an area of shallow, stagnant water, and contrary to typical otter behavior, it was allowing people to approach it without fleeing. That was a clear sign to the rescue center staff that the animal was in trouble. By nine o'clock that evening, photographs and videos of the otter had been shared with biologists from Fisheries and Oceans Canada, rescue center manager Lindsay Akhurst, and aquarium veterinarian Martin Haulena, all of whom agreed that the animal needed to be retrieved.

Sea otters aren't the typical animal that the aquarium rescues. Since the program was established in the 1960s, it has responded to about 150 calls each year to collect and rehabilitate marine mammals, but the overwhelming majority are young harbor seals that have become separated from their mothers in the first weeks or months of their lives. There are numerous reasons why harbor seal pups may need to be rescued, from first-time moms not knowing how to care for them to injuries caused by human activities. And the rescue center has a permit from the Canadian government to respond to such calls whenever necessary. The center also regularly responds to stranded or injured harbor porpoises, elephant seals, and sea lions, and in recent years it has even begun to go into the field to disentangle marine mammals, mostly sea lions, that have become caught up in fishing gear. But it had responded to only one sea otter call before the Tofino animal, and that was a year before in Washington State. That animal was found to have massive liver failure, and it died soon after it was collected.

"We're basically a facility that responds to a public need," explained Haulena. "We don't go out looking for animals, but we always respond when someone calls us to do something."

So the next day the rescue center dispatched two teams of personnel to collect the animal. One team had planned to fly the 180 miles to the coastal resort community, but the plane was fogged in and never left the airport. The second team, which included Akhurst, went by car and ferry, a nearly six-hour trip. It was sunset by the time they got there, but an officer from Fisheries and Oceans was standing by at the rocky shoreline keeping an eye on the male otter they later named Walter. He didn't look good. Walter was hardly noticeable, hidden between two docks and amid piles of seaweed, sticks, and detritus. Since no healthy sea otter would submit to being in those conditions, the rescue center team was even more determined in their assignment.

Given his poor health, Walter was easy to capture. Wearing a headlamp in the near darkness, the Fisheries and Oceans officer distracted the otter from one side while Akhurst snuck in from behind with a large hoop net and scooped him up. Although the animal initially tried to swim away, he was far too weak to escape and was easily placed in a portable kennel for the trip back to Vancouver. Because sea otters can easily overheat when out of the water, Akhurst stopped several times during the return trip to purchase a total of twenty-five bags of ice to put inside the kennel to keep Walter cool.

Arriving back at the rescue center at two in the morning, Walter was guided into an enclosure and pool and provided with what may have been his first healthy meal in days. During the next forty-eight hours he received round-the-clock care, including intravenous fluids, pain medication, and antibiotics to stabilize him. The full extent of his wounds was still mostly unknown.

THE VANCOUVER AQUARIUM'S marine mammal rescue center sits behind a green fence on the city's waterfront and consists of an office trailer, several sheds where examinations and surgeries take place, and a number of outdoor pools of various sizes for holding and rehabilitating marine mammals. Two days after the otter's rescue, veterinarian Haulena and his technicians anesthetized Walter and conducted a thorough examination. He was in worse shape than they imagined. Walter was severely malnourished; he had a badly fractured flipper, numerous shattered teeth, and tenderness in his shoulder; and both eyes had been perforated, rendering him blind. X-rays showed the cause of his problems: he had been shot with a shotgun and had dozens of pellets embedded throughout his body. Due to his dense fur, no one had noticed the pellet injuries. Additional tests found liver and metabolic problems, probably from not having eaten much over an extended period.

"It was quite a shock to us all to find that he was shot, that his injuries were human caused," Akhurst said sadly. "We initially wondered if he was just an older otter who was declining from natural causes, which made us wonder if we should even intervene.

But once we realized that humans were involved, we switched gears to do everything in our power."

Over the course of the next six weeks, Walter's round-the-clock care continued. Only two shotgun pellets were removed from his body, because most of the entrance wounds had healed over, but he had two toes and part of his right flipper amputated. An oral surgeon also removed three broken teeth and conducted a complex root canal to save one of the animal's canine teeth. Walter gained eleven pounds during that time on a healthy diet of shrimp, clams, and crab, and he was back to spending much of his day grooming himself.

When I visited the rescue center on a snowy December day less than two months after Walter's rescue, the facility was somewhat quiet. While it has at times housed more than one hundred rehabilitating animals at once, that day there were fewer than a dozen, almost all harbor seals. When I first arrived, I found Walter sleeping on a wooden platform at the edge of his eight-foot wide pool. The coffee-colored fur on his head and upper body blended smoothly into the chocolate brown of his lower body, and a quick glance confirmed that his coat was still thick and lush. I would not have guessed that he was injured or sickly in any way.

As I watched, he slid into the water and began to roll—a behavior Gavin Maxwell described in his classic British memoir *Ring of Bright Water* as a "pirouette in the horizontal plane, like a chicken on a spit that has gone mad"—before stopping briefly to use both front paws to groom his face in the exact manner that I wash my own face. Then he rolled in the water some more, pulled himself halfway out of the tank and gave himself a quick shake to rid his head of water, then dived back in and began rolling some more. He groomed his belly, moved on to his tail, rubbing it repeatedly with both paws, then returned to his face, ears, and eyes. At times it looked like he was grooming his scalp just like people rub shampoo into their hair.

This grooming behavior continued for my entire twenty-minute visit, shifting from head to belly to tail and back again, with more rolling in the water in between each grooming cycle. Haulena said that captive sea otters generally do only three things—eat, sleep, and groom. I had by then observed two out of three, and while I didn't stay long enough to watch Walter being fed, it was apparently a simple and entertaining process. As soon as he heard a caretaker enter his enclosure, Walter asked for food by slapping his chest with his paws. Food was then tossed on his chest as he reclined on his back in the water, and when he finished, he slapped his chest for more. Despite his blindness, Walter learned well how to quickly retrieve any food items that dropped from his chest.

Although Walter recovered from most of his horrific wounds, it was obvious that he would never be released back into the wild. Haulena said that rehabilitated animals are good candidates for release only if they are not a danger to people or other free-ranging wildlife, if they are free of pain and able to forage on their own, and if they can avoid predators as adeptly as animals that have not gone through rehabilitation. Because of his blindness, Walter failed on the last point. So eleven weeks after his rescue, Walter was put on exhibit at the Vancouver Aquarium alongside three long-term resident otters that had been transferred there from the Alaska SeaLife Center. According to Haulena, Walter was an ideal animal for display because he told an important story about the impact humans have on wildlife, not only the unintentional effects of human activities but, in this case, the intentional harm as well. Sadly, Walter died in his sleep in December 2015 after two years in captivity. He was believed to have been about fifteen years old when he died, which is the average lifespan of a sea otter in the wild.

Public reaction to the cause of Walter's injuries was overwhelming, with justifiably angry comments and wild speculation appearing on social media and in the news. Unfortunately, Walter isn't the only sea otter that is intentionally harmed by disturbed individuals who apparently find joy in causing senseless injury and death to innocent animals. Jim Curland at Friends of the Sea Otter calls acts of cruelty against sea otters "heinous crimes" that are "incomprehensible to those of us who love animals." He says that such acts are pretty rare—typically fewer than half a dozen each year are reported in California and less than one a year in British Columbia—but he worries about how many shootings go unreported because the animals are never found.

"The only way we find out is if they wash up on the beach or they are found floating in the water," he said. "We hear that some are weighted down so the evidence never surfaces. This kind of violence might happen more often than we know about, especially in more remote areas."

Curland points to the sad events of early September 2013, when three male sea otters were shot and found dead along Asilomar State Beach in Pacific Grove, California, on the Monterey peninsula. Two were shot in the head and one was shot in the back with coated lead bullets. The US Fish and Wildlife Service conducted a criminal investigation, but it wasn't until five months later that it publicized the crime and sought help in finding the perpetrators. A $21,000 reward was offered for information leading to an arrest and conviction, but so far nothing of substance has come of it. But there has been a great deal of speculation about who could do such a thing.

Most of that speculation focuses on fishermen, who are clearly unhappy with the affect that sea otters have on their ability to make a living. Fishermen appear to be the only ones with a financial incentive to kill otters and the only ones likely to get frustrated enough with the popular animals to overreact and shoot some of the offending otters. But no one in any official capacity is willing to publicly accuse anyone in the fishing community of the crimes without solid evidence. In fact, when I asked Curland to speculate, he was very diplomatic and went out of his way to avoid saying that he thought fishermen were involved.

"Whenever we're asked by the media if this is a case of frustrated fishermen, our answer is 'it could be,'" he said. "But we don't want to make a blanket statement that it has to be a fisherman. . . . We don't want to taint all fishermen. It could be a fisherman, but it could be some other disturbed individual. Or it could just be vandals. It's just incomprehensible to be taking potshots at animals for the fun of it."

Since sea otters are protected by the US Endangered Species Act and the Marine Mammal Protection Act, anyone (other than Native Alaskans) convicted of killing an otter in the United States faces significant fines and potential jail time. In British Columbia, where sea otters are listed as a species of special concern, perpetrators would face similar consequences. One of the few recent cases of an individual being prosecuted for such crimes occurred in Moss Landing, California, in 2015, when a man was sentenced to 150 hours of community service, a $500 fine, and six months of probation for shooting a baby sea otter with an air rifle. The man's justification, which I found ridiculous, was that the otter had been crying for weeks—not likely—and he was annoyed listening to it. Although the animal was not killed in the incident, the man was still convicted.

WALTER AND EVERY OTHER sea otter in British Columbia are descended from otters from Alaska that were translocated to the province between 1969 and 1972. Sea otters had been extirpated from the province during the fur trade, with the last one reportedly shot in 1931. Plenty of suitable habitat was available up and down the outer coast of Vancouver Island when the decision was made by Fisheries and Oceans Canada and the British Columbia Fish and Wildlife Branch to reestablish a sea otter population in the province. In July of 1969, biologists from British Columbia and the Alaska Department of Fish and Game transported thirty otters captured at Amchitka Island to Checleset Bay, on the northwest coast of Vancouver Island, for release. The trip was a stressful one, with multiple stops and transfers to other planes, and one otter died in transit. Few of the others lived long after being released, probably due to the trying circumstances of their journey.

So in 1970 the government biologists tried again. This time they brought forty-five otters from Prince William Sound, Alaska, to Checleset Bay via ship, a six-day, storm-tossed trip during which many of the otters died from the stress. Just fourteen of the forty-five animals were alive to be released, and little is known about their fate. Officials tried one last time to reintroduce sea otters to British Columbia in 1972, when forty-seven animals were flown from Prince William Sound to Vancouver Island. Upon arrival at Checleset Bay, they were placed in floating holding pens and fed for several days to acclimate them to their new surroundings. Just one of the animals, a female pup, died in the process, and the rest were released in what was believed to be healthy condition.

Although a total of eighty-nine sea otters were released in the bay during the three reintroduction efforts, by 1973 the population contained as few as twenty-eight animals, probably because most of them dispersed elsewhere or died. But those that survived were officially protected by a regulation in Canada's Federal Fisheries Act in 1970 and by the British Columbia Wildlife Act in 1996. In 1981, an ecological reserve was created to encompass thirty-three square miles of Checleset Bay to further protect the sea otter colony. Those efforts, and the natural dispersal of the sea otters, succeeded in quickly growing the otter population. By 1977, sea otters had colonized the west side of Nootka Island, forty-five miles to the south of Checleset Bay, but none were found in between. During the next eighteen years, the British Columbia sea otter population grew at 19 percent per year and then at 8.4 percent per year for the thirteen years after that, spreading throughout much of the west side of Vancouver Island, from Clayoquot Sound in the south up around the north end of the island to Queen Charlotte Strait. A raft of otters was even discovered in 1989 at Goose Island, on the central coast of the province, seventy-five miles north of the rest of the population, and that group had expanded another fifty-five miles north to Aristazabal Island by 2013. Today, more than 5,600 sea otters live in the waters around Vancouver Island, and another 1,000 reside on the central British Columbia coast.

To find out more about this population of sea otters, I flew by floatplane from Gold River Inlet on an uneventful fifteen-minute flight to Friendly Cove at the tiny historic village of Yuquot, the southwesternmost point of Nootka Island, a 206-square-mile landmass centrally located along the west coast of Vancouver Island. I went there to meet Roger Dunlop, a biologist for the Uu-a-thluk/Nuu-chah-nulth Tribal Council, to conduct a sea otter survey of

Nootka Island aboard his thirty-two-foot sailboat *Merango*, but he hadn't arrived yet. I knew the unpredictable winds made it difficult to keep a sailboat on any sort of schedule, so I wasn't surprised. When the boat moored in the cove two hours later, Dunlop said he had been fighting a headwind for most of the way.

Born in London and raised mostly in Canada, Dunlop worked in the oil industry before pursuing a career in marine biology and wildlife management. For nearly twenty-five years he has worked for the tribal council, which governs about 9,500 First Nations people from fourteen tribes along a two-hundred-mile stretch of Vancouver Island coastline from the Brooks Peninsula south to Port Renfrew. While he focuses most of his attention on studying and managing the region's salmon fishery, Dunlop also pays close attention to the sea otter population, which some tribal members complain is in direct competition with the tribes for food. He participates in Canada's sea otter recovery process and conducts regular otter surveys, but he is in the sometimes-uncomfortable position of advocating for the needs of the tribal council while also ensuring that the otter population remains healthy. Despite having no blood relation to the First Nations people, the fair-skinned Dunlop was dubbed "Uupiihaa" by the tribal council, a name he says means "person who helps a lot."

We remained anchored in Friendly Cove for the night to await an expected change in the wind that would determine what direction we would take around Nootka Island the following day. So Dunlop took me on a brief walking tour of the village to meet some of the tribal members who were beginning their annual campout on the island.

It was apropos that we met at Friendly Cove because that's where Europeans made first contact with the First Nations on the

Pacific coast of British Columbia and triggered the trade in sea otter furs. Captain Cook landed in the tiny cove in 1778 and traded with the powerful Chief Maquinna for sea otter pelts that were later sold in China for an exorbitant price. The village soon became a battleground between the Spanish and English, who both sought to control the territory and the fur trade along with it. A Spanish settlement and fort were eventually erected there in the 1780s and later abandoned, rebuilt, and abandoned again after the three Nootka Sound Conventions helped avert war between Spain and England. Maquinna and his people later reoccupied the village, which continued to be important to the fur trade. Even after the sea otter population was wiped out in nearby waters, pelts from great distances away were still brought to Friendly Cove to be traded by Maquinna to the merchants, who the First Nations called the Bostonauts. In 1802, Maquinna and his villagers massacred the crew of the ship *Boston*, keeping the only two survivors as slaves for three years. But as sea otters became more and more difficult to find in the area, Yuquot and Friendly Cove no longer played a central role in the fur trade.

THE NEXT MORNING we began our circumnavigation of Nootka Island, whose name means "go around, go around" in the Nuu-chah-nulth language. We began by following the outer coast north toward the First Nations village of Nuchatlitz, an area where sea otters are known to be abundant, but we observed few otters along the way. Initially, we made little progress in calm winds and saw just two otters in the distance in our first two hours. But as we approached Bajo Point, where a rocky reef lies just offshore, the wind picked up rapidly and we sped past the reef. We were going so fast that we barely got a glimpse of the sea otters that were foraging in the area. Large waves crashed over the reef, and I was bouncing around in the boat with little ability to scan the water with my binoculars. I believe I saw six animals scattered in pairs amid the kelp on either side of the reef, but I couldn't be sure. It was my first indication that conducting a sea otter survey from a sailboat was not likely going to generate results that could be relied upon by the scientific community.

When we finally reached Ferrer Point, the entrance to the southern tip of Nuchatlitz Inlet, Dunlop announced that we were "coming into mom-and-pup central," where he has annually counted hundreds of sea otter mothers and their young. Located at the northwest corner of Nootka Island, the entire area is part of Nuchatlitz Provincial Park, home to the Nuchatlaht people, and consists of an archipelago of about one hundred islands (and even more at low tide). The entrance to the wide inlet was clogged with guided recreational boats fishing for the large and abundant salmon that traverse the region.

We lowered the sail and motored to a protected cove, where we moored and took a tiny rubber dinghy to Nuchatlitz Island, to walk the shore at low tide and search for signs of sea otters. What we found was a wide sand flat covered with mussel, butter clam, and cockle shells—almost all empty—along with a number of fist-size horse clam shells with distinctive holes in the middle that were probably made by a sea otter cracking them open with a rock.

At dawn the next morning, Dunlop and I loaded life preservers, cameras, binoculars, and waterproof data sheets into the dinghy and began a sea otter survey of Nuchatlitz Inlet and the bulk of the archipelago. We headed first for a rocky island about one hundred feet in circumference, near where Dunlop said a raft of mothers and pups are often observed, that would give us a proper vantage point for scanning the region for otters. We tossed a grappling hook to the mussel-covered rocks to secure the boat, then stumbled out and climbed hand over hand to the pinnacle. Although we were just thirty feet above the water's surface, the view of the dozen nearby islets was impressive. The large raft of female otters and their pups that Dunlop was expecting to see on the other side of the island was nowhere in sight. Instead, a smaller raft of thirty-nine males kept an eye on us as we counted an additional nineteen otters scattered widely over the area. We saw at least three more rafts of otters in the distance, but we waited to get closer before attempting to count them.

For the next three hours we toured the archipelago as the weather deteriorated and the wind picked up. Dunlop thought nothing of blasting through the waves, but I found it difficult to watch for otters without risking getting thrown into the soup. Yet sea otters were everywhere. We saw three rafts of mother-pup pairs totaling eighty-four animals near Ensenada Island, a similar raft of sixty-seven mother-pup pairs at Justice Island, and smaller numbers at Port Langford, Ferrer Point, and numerous unnamed sites. We found otters scattered widely throughout the inlet and archipelago, even in areas where Dunlop seldom sees them. Small rafts of males turned up in several unexpected places, like near the outermost islands and Nuchatlitz Reef, where the wind and water conditions were so rough I could do nothing but hold on. Dunlop, though, was skilled at maintaining lists of numbers in his head as we traveled, stopping only occasionally to write them down before moving on to the next area.

While most of the otter groups we observed appeared to be mother-and-pup pairs, it was sometimes difficult to draw that conclusion because many of the pups were nearly as large as their mothers and were no longer resting on their moms' bellies. Yet when we approached them, the otter pairs often reunited to gawk at us.

One pair was particularly bold—or maybe just oblivious to us. Mom wasn't especially attentive to her pup, and her youngster behaved as if it was nearly ready to be on its own. Still exhibiting some fluffier fur from its natal pelage, the pup strayed a few yards from its mother, seemingly testing out its swimming and diving abilities, but quickly popped back to the surface and immediately glanced around to be sure mom wasn't too far away. After briefly making eye contact with her, the pup strayed a little farther, until its mother appeared to decide that it had wandered far enough and slowly backstroked to retrieve it. After a quick bout of grooming, the pup began the process again. It clearly thought it was ready for its independence.

An accidental revving of our outboard motor briefly alarmed the animals, however, and most of the oversize pups returned to their mothers' sides, including the one we had been watching. Maybe it wasn't ready for independence after all. It tried to climb aboard its mother's belly for some added security, but it was too big and slipped off the other side, making me laugh out loud and alarm the animals further. With a little yank from mom, the pup finally balanced on its mother's belly as she paddled them away to a safer distance. Mom then attempted to groom her not-so-little one, scratching its chest and neck with her paws, but they couldn't maintain their balance long and eventually gave up the effort. After staring at Dunlop and me for a few moments, they decided it was safe to go about their activities, so the pup began another round of exercising its independence. That was our signal to move on.

By the end of the morning, we tallied 418 adult sea otters and 304 pups, which was less than half the usual number Dunlop records in the area. We were unable to survey the entire basin, though, and the animals were more widely scattered than Dunlop usually sees, so it is unlikely we saw them all, especially given the conditions.

We departed Nuchatlitz in midafternoon and picked up a good breeze to carry us east along the calm Esperanza Channel, then turned south on Hecate Channel, where the wind died and we slowed and glided by three salmon farms and little else. The channels separating Nootka from Vancouver Island are less than a mile wide but up to nine hundred feet deep in places, thanks to the area's geological history as a fjord carved by glaciers. The waters well offshore were far shallower than the protected channels. Sea otters were scarce in the channels, however. Dunlop said that five years earlier a raft of about fifty otters moved slowly through the channels, exploiting the little available food before returning to the outer coast. It took us four hours to cruise the last three miles to the town of Tahsis, where we stayed the night and I caught the floatplane for home, while Dunlop planned to continue sailing for several more weeks.

BEFORE THE FUR TRADE, many of the approximately twenty thousand First Nations people who lived in tribal villages around Nootka Sound were expert sea otter hunters, but the pelts became the sole possession of the highest-ranking chiefs, who wore otter-skin robes and anklets to signify their rank. Dunlop called such attire "the crown jewels" of the tribe. The fur trade led to a collapse of that societal practice because individual hunters often sneaked off to trade or sell otter skins without having to give them to the chief.

According to Dunlop, the fur trade also triggered a significant change in the diet of the local tribes. In an archaeological excavation of a traditional refuse heap, or midden, at Friendly Cove, scientists revealed a distinct layer in the midden that corresponds to the time when sea otters disappeared from the area. "Prior to 1792 and for about four or five thousand years before that, the midden is dominated by hard-shelled animals like barnacles, snails, and all kinds of small mollusks," Dunlop said. "But after 1792, clams became dominant." He believes this is a clear indication of the influence of sea otters on the diet of these First Nations peoples.

Prior to the fur trade and their disappearance, the sea otters would have suppressed the population of clams, urchins, and other large invertebrates through their own foraging. That left the less appealing hard-shelled mollusks for the Natives to collect and eat. But when sea otters became extirpated, the apex predator no longer kept populations of the larger invertebrates in check, allowing them to expand dramatically and leading to a change in the diet of the tribes. Now that sea otters have returned to the area and are competing with the First Nations people for those same large invertebrates, Dunlop thinks the tribes should consider returning to some of their historic foods.

"It's been more than two hundred years, so the people have probably forgotten what foods were very prevalent back in the day when there were sea otters here," he said. "The midden at Friendly Cove before 1792 will give you a picture of what people were eating at that time." He calls them "otter-proof foods" because they were species that sea otters could not easily break open, like red turban snails and moon snails. "There are many, many more species of mollusks, large gastropods, or snails that are out there that I think people have forgotten were once part of their diet. If you think about it that way, it's easier to accept the change that comes in the ecology out here from having sea otters and kelp." But Dunlop hasn't had much success convincing the tribes to rethink their diets. He said he "got some pretty shocking dismissals" when he suggested it in Alaska, though he believes that some recognize that the idea makes sense.

Perhaps the First Nations people's resistance to the idea spawns from the fact that the tribes were not consulted when sea otters were reintroduced to the region in the 1970s. A decision was made, a site was selected, and the animals were dropped off without any communication with those who would be affected. I would have been pretty unhappy about that, too. Although there was little initial backlash by the tribes back then, there is considerable resentment today when they see protected otters eating food they think should be their own. "Some people have hundreds of sea otters in their front yard and they're not allowed to disturb them," Dunlop said.

A management plan Dunlop is preparing for the tribal council is not going to address the issue of competition. Instead, it aims to allow the tribes to establish a sea otter hunt with the goal of rein-stating their custom of wearing their ceremonial regalia. Dunlop said the plan will likely recommend a "ceremonial harvest" of about sixty to seventy animals per year from across the British Columbia population so no subgroup is adversely affected.

Although the plan is far from complete and isn't a priority for the tribal council, just talking about it is raising red flags among wildlife enthusiasts. Whenever the subject comes up, Dunlop envisions headlines reading "otter slaughter" that do not accurately reflect what will likely be proposed. Which may be one reason why the tribes are still discussing the idea and an otter hunt is not on the horizon. "The people who oppose any kind of sea otter management are those that don't live in close proximity to the animals and don't have their way of life disrupted," Dunlop said. "I think the people here have been extremely tolerant of these animals. The burden of that tolerance falls on the people here who can't get their customary foods very easily anymore."

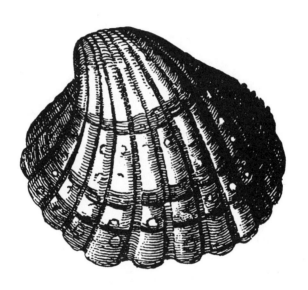

Chapter 13: Gaining Ground

ALTHOUGH SEA OTTERS are best known for living in rocky, kelp-dominated habitat, where they play a key role in the maintenance of the ecosystem, that is not the only habitat where they're found. About 25 percent of the habitat in the central part of their California range is soft, sandy sediment with little or no kelp. The long, smooth coastlines of Pismo Beach and Estero Bay, as well as nearly the entire stretch of coast from Monterey to Santa Cruz, are sandy embayments, and sea otters are found there, too. That's typically where the nonterritorial males hang out in large groups, feeding on fat innkeeper worms and burrowing clams and what Tim Tinker calls "episodically abundant prey" like Dungeness crabs, sand dollars, and squid. These prey items are episodically abundant because they are available to the otters only during short windows of time when the creatures move closer to shore during their breeding season. There may be resting groups of eighty to one hundred male sea otters gathered together in sandy habitat, but seldom will a mother and pup be among them. A few juvenile and subadult females may be mixed in with the males, but those have not yet begun to breed. Once they do, the females usually limit themselves to the food-rich areas of the kelp forest.

Sea otter density is quite low in soft-sediment habitats, with an average of just two otters per square kilometer compared to five or six in rocky habitat—and twice that in the uniquely productive area of the Monterey peninsula. Otter density is also more variable in sandy habitat because it tends to be an otter travel zone, as mobile males come and go from season to season, tracking the episodically available prey from place to place. On a cold fall morning whale-watching excursion north from Monterey, I traveled more than a dozen miles along the sandy habitat of coastal Monterey Bay before seeing my first sea otters. When the first whales came into view just off the town of Moss Landing, several dozen sea otters were resting and feeding there, too. They were perched at the edge of the nutrient-rich Monterey Canyon, an underwater canyon that extends ninety-three miles offshore and reaches depths of nearly twelve thousand feet. At the mouth of the canyon is Elkhorn Slough, a narrow tidal estuary that divides the town of Moss Landing. It's the only estuary within the range of the southern sea otter. And it's there that the otters are just beginning to reveal another element of their remarkable ecological influence.

Located about halfway between Monterey and Santa Cruz, Moss Landing is a quiet village on Highway 1 in the Salinas Valley, an important area for the commercial production of fruits and vegetables. When I visited, the large farm stands in town were selling artichokes and grapefruits at ten for a dollar, and avocados at seven for a dollar, prices far below what I've ever seen anywhere in the East in my lifetime. The most prominent feature of the community, besides the natural gas–fired power plant and its two massive concrete smokestacks, is Elkhorn Slough. At its inlet to the bay, a marina and yacht club share space with small businesses renting kayaks to tourists, while most of the inland properties surrounding the slough are protected by private conservation groups and the Elkhorn Slough National Estuarine Research Reserve. Although the community may be best known beyond the immediate region as the home of the Monterey Bay Aquarium Research Institute and the Moss Landing Marine Laboratories, the slough dominates its geography and culture.

Unfortunately, Elkhorn Slough is the destination for large quantities of polluted runoff from the adjacent farmlands and roadways, negatively affecting the health of the waterway. Nutrients in the runoff fuel massive algae blooms that suck the oxygen from the water and impair water quality, making it, according to Tinker, the most unhealthy estuary in the state. Yet because the slough is tidal, enabling clean ocean water from Monterey Canyon to flush the pollutants from the slough, it continues to host an enormous abundance of wildlife, including more than a dozen species of shorebirds, hundreds of California sea lions and harbor seals, and a growing complement of sea otters.

Until early 2014, rafts of seventy to ninety sea otters—mostly males, but also a few subadult females—were regularly observed from the marina and kayak launch just inside the seawall protecting the entrance to the slough. Several months later, however, most had moved a mile or so deeper into the slough, probably because of recent episodes of shark predation. On my visit, just two subadult males were observed at the entrance, wrestling with each other like ten-year-old boys, pushing and slapping and grabbing and grunting as they rolled over and over together in what appeared to be gleeful play.

I was there with Tinker and three young otter biologists as they conducted an informal assessment of Elkhorn Slough's otter population and attempted to identify previously tagged otters.

Traveling aboard the US Geological Survey vessel *Pursuit*, we passed a dock covered with nearly fifty noisy sea lions, cruised beneath the bridge carrying Highway 1, and proceeded down the main channel into the slough. It was high tide, so the abundant eelgrass on either side of the channel was barely visible, but harbor seals were lounging on the banks, willets and elegant terns called out loudly as they flew parallel to our route, and monarch butterflies, which winter in enormous aggregations in trees just a few miles up the coast, slowly floated overhead.

Tinker says that sea otters use the variable habitat in the slough in different ways. Large mollusks are abundant in the main channel and can be an important source of protein for the otters, but they require considerable digging to unearth, so they are often not the preferred prey. The eelgrass beds that grow in dense canopies along the banks of the first mile or two of the slough—which previously had only survived in tiny patches before the sea otters moved into the area—provide nursery habitat for fish and a place for crabs and invertebrates to hide, so otters can often find a meal there. When sea otters first became resident in the slough around 2001, they confined themselves to the first half mile of the waterway, where they consumed most of the fist-size rock crabs and the smaller invasive green crabs. But as otter numbers grew, they expanded deeper and deeper into the slough to take advantage of different prey and habitats.

As we approached Seal Bend, where a large raft of male otters regularly congregated in late 2014, biologist Sarah Espinosa set up a tall antenna, turned on a radio receiver, and dialed in the frequencies of the seventeen resident otters (out of approximately eighty total residing there) that have been implanted with transmitters. Every day, a team of volunteers visits the slough to locate each of the otters and assess its behavior and activities. The first tagged otter we detected was identified as Otter 3421, a subadult female who we found a few hundred yards from the raft of males. A steady beeping noise from the receiver indicated she was resting at the surface, but then the sound stopped, probably because she had dived beneath the surface, where the transmitter cannot be detected. When she popped to the surface again, we heard one loud beep before the quiet steady pulse resumed.

Glancing ashore at Seal Bend, we saw two volunteer otter spotters using high-powered telescopes and an antenna-and-receiver setup like the one we were using on the boat. They counted forty-four otters in the raft, all drifting with the current and then swimming upstream en masse to rest and drift some more before repeating the process. The otters were trying to remain in their preferred section of Seal Bend, a two-hundred-yard-wide strip of eelgrass, but with the strong current and no kelp to hold onto, they found it necessary to repeatedly swim upstream to maintain their place. With every tagged otter the spotters found, they noted its location, behaviors, and a wide variety of other information. Determining the otter's exact position in the slough is especially important, because when combined with other data, it indicates the specific habitat it is using, which helps the scientists establish the demands placed on different sites. In addition to the data collected every day of the year by the volunteers, biologists like Espinosa regularly spend up to twelve hours at a time watching one individual otter to establish its activity budget—everything it does throughout the day, from the location and length of its foraging dives to the prey it consumes and the tools it uses to open its prey. "It's very unique to have an animal in the marine environment that will go down and bring its food to the surface to show us. That's how we have this amazing data set of foraging that doesn't exist for any other marine species," said Brent Hughes, a University of California, Santa Cruz, doctoral student.

Hughes is the one who made the surprising discovery about the role that sea otters play in the maintenance of the health of this estuary ecosystem. Biologists hadn't paid much attention when the sea otters moved into Elkhorn Slough in the 1980s, or when the animals disappeared for a short time in the late 1990s. The otters were mostly males, and they initially were not year-round residents, but when they returned in the early 2000s, they were joined by some females and established a permanent subpopulation. But Hughes wasn't interested in the otters. He was studying the eelgrass, the long ribbonlike green stems of seagrass that grow in extensive beds in sandy substrate; like kelp, eelgrass is home to an abundance of invertebrates and serves as nursery grounds for many species of fish and other marine creatures.

As in every other estuary on the West Coast, the Elkhorn Slough eelgrass beds had been in a steady state of decline for many years. Hughes could see it from early aerial photographs and from measurements other scientists had taken for several decades. As fertilizers and other runoff from nearby farmlands found their way into the slough, those nutrients caused an increase in algae, which attached to the eelgrass blades, denying them access to sunlight and choking the life out of them. It's a process called eutrophication, a natural phenomenon in some lakes but a result of pollution in estuaries. When Hughes went to Elkhorn Slough to make measurements of the eelgrass beds, expecting to find continuing eutrophication, he instead saw healthy new growth and lots of tiny microorganisms grazing the algae off the eelgrass blades. "The seagrass was really green and thriving where there were lots of sea otters, even compared to seagrass in more pristine systems without excess nutrients," he said. So he gathered as much historic data about the slough as he could find from other researchers—crab population numbers, sea otter diet data, nutrient levels, and more—and it told a completely unexpected story.

He found that the species that were primarily in control of the slough habitat prior to the arrival of the sea otters were crabs, especially the large number of rock crabs. As they crawled along on the muddy floor of the slough, they ate most of the numerous bottom-feeding invertebrates, including a sea slug called the California sea hare, which feeds primarily on algae. Without these grazing invertebrates around to eat the algae off the eelgrass, the eelgrass became suffocated. But when the otters arrived in the slough in the 1980s, the crab population declined, the invertebrate population increased, and the eelgrass began to get healthier. During those few years in the 1990s when the otters left the slough again, the whole process began to reverse itself—the crabs gained in numbers, the invertebrates declined, and the algae smothered the eelgrass. Now that the otters have returned in even bigger numbers and are staying around all year, the eelgrass is the healthiest it has been in quite some time.

This four-level cascade—from sea otters to crabs to algae-grazing invertebrates to eelgrass—has turned Elkhorn Slough's eelgrass beds into the healthiest of any estuary on the West Coast. And it is all because Elkhorn Slough is the only estuary on the West Coast that has a population of sea otters. There are plenty of other tidal estuaries that are undergoing expensive eelgrass restoration efforts and could benefit from the animals. Many, including the entire San Francisco Bay area, have archaeological evidence of historic populations of otters prior to the fur trade. Tinker said these estuaries may, over time, become vitally important as sea otters expand their range north and south. "Sea otters have improved the health and abundance of eelgrass beds in a way that no one in a million years would have predicted," he said. "And the only way we ever would have found it was to study it as it happened. All of a sudden we have another keystone story in a totally different environment, one that no one saw coming."

And it may not be the last keystone story that sea otters have to tell.

AFTER SINKING INTO the mud to our shins while climbing out of the *Pursuit* to scan the slough, we walked a short distance into the adjacent salt marsh, where Hughes had established experimental plots to assess the effect that otters have on marsh habitat. The abundant algae blooms have caused a spike in purple-lined shore crabs, a crab with a blackish carapace blending to pinkish claws that feeds on the algae. But the crabs burrow into the banks of the slough and create what Hughes calls "crab condominiums," destabilizing the banks and causing increasing erosion. Hughes found that the resident otters are now feeding on the crabs and improving the condition of the salt marsh. "Where there are crabs, it looks like gophers have invaded your lawn—lots of holes from crab burrows eating away at the soil," Hughes said.

"Four years ago we didn't believe the benefit otters provide to eelgrass, and now we're finding it hard to believe the influence otters have on the salt marsh," Tinker added.

Tinker is right to be impressed by what is being discovered about the resiliency of sea otters and the influence the animals have on their environment. It makes it easy to feel optimistic about their future. They have survived a great deal already—the devastating fur trade, significant diseases in various parts of their range, food limitation and shark-bite mortality in California, killer whales in Alaska, competition with fishermen of all varieties—and yet they are still expanding their range and growing in abundance in many places. But that is not to say that additional threats aren't lurking. The warming climate is one factor that is raising major red flags for many species and ecosystems around the globe, and yet its likely effects on sea otters are unknown. Sea otters prefer cold waters, so as the oceans warm the otters' range may shift northward. But even that is uncertain. As the land warms, winds off the sea will likely intensify, driving an upwelling of cold waters from the deep into the sea otters' coastal environment. That may keep the water cool enough so sea otters don't have to move northward after all, at least not any time soon.

The greater concern is a potential decline of otter prey due to ocean acidification. As carbon dioxide concentrations in the atmosphere increase and mix into the ocean, seawater becomes more acidic, making it more difficult for shelled organisms to produce the calcium carbonate they use to build their shells. And since most of what sea otters eat has some sort of shell—clams, crabs, urchins—a decline in those species could have serious implications for otters.

Biologist Verena Gill may be the otter scientist most worried about climate-related threats to sea otters. She speculates that warming waters may force otter prey species to seek refuge in water too deep for sea otters to reach them on the bottom. She's concerned that an increase in storm intensity and changes in ocean circulation may shift the populations of plankton that feed the clams that otters eat. And she worries that more intense storms may kill more pups or separate them from their mothers or bring novel diseases into their range.

"We're just starting to grapple with what it will mean," she said. "Are otters adaptable enough to change their prey? Maybe. But could they sustain themselves on it? I don't know."

Gill's concern about the arrival of novel diseases as waters warm may already be realized. In the fall of 2015, more than three hundred sea otters mysteriously died and washed ashore in Kachemak Bay, Alaska, and most were determined to have died from an unknown bacterial infection. While fifty to one hundred sea otters in that area typically die each year from similar causes, the increase in 2015 had scientists speculating that something else was contributing to the otter deaths—perhaps another disease or a toxin from harmful algae blooms, either of which could have arrived in what many scientists were calling "a blob of warm water" that had spread throughout the region.

While the possible threats to sea otters from climate change are still mostly unknown, the greater threat may be one we already know a great deal about—oil spills. The Exxon Valdez spill in Prince William Sound, in the heart of their range in Alaska, killed as many as three thousand otters in 1989, and it took twenty-five years for the population there to recover. A significant oil spill along the central California coast could wipe out the entire population of southern sea otters. The animals lucked out in 2015 when 105,000 gallons of oil spilled from an underground pipeline that ruptured in Santa Barbara County and ran into the ocean just a few miles from the southernmost point of the sea otter range. No otters were harmed, but if it had happened a little farther north, it could have been devastating.

According to Laird Henkel, director of the Marine Wildlife Veterinary Care and Research Center of the California Office of Spill Prevention and Response, just a dime-size spot of oil on a sea otter is the equivalent of a hole in a diver's wet suit, allowing cold water to rush in and disrupt the waterproofing abilities of the otter's fur coat. The animal quickly becomes hypothermic, loses its buoyancy, and hauls out of the water to try to warm up. Then the otter begins grooming itself, causing the toxic oil to become ingested and leading to all sorts of nasty issues, from gastrointestinal lesions and organ failure to respiratory problems and burns on the skin. If the oil doesn't kill the animal quickly, it certainly decreases its long-term survival.

The one good thing that came from the Exxon Valdez spill, however, was a much-needed focus on oil-spill prevention, readiness, and research, including the establishment of the Oiled Wildlife Care Network in California and the construction of a dozen facilities around the state where oiled otters and other animals can be cleaned and rehabilitated. A research project even investigated the best way to clean an oiled sea otter—an hour of washing the animal with Dawn dishwashing detergent, an hour of rinsing, then drying with towels and a blow dryer, followed by soaking in a pool of warm, softened freshwater.

The oiled otter rehab facility in Santa Cruz that Henkel manages was built to care for 125 otters, and floating net pens are available to house otters in harbors along the coast while they wait for their home territories to be cleaned. While he plans for the worst-case scenario of dozens of oiled otters arriving at his facility for days at a time, Henkel said that just one otter has required the facility's services since it opened in 1997—an animal that found fame as Olive the Oiled Otter, and succeeded in raising three pups after being cleaned and released.

"Any oil going into the water is bad for wildlife," said Henkel. "The oil-spill risk is decreasing because there's now more and more regulation. The transition to double-hulled cargo ships has helped. So has the establishment of marine sanctuaries, which pushed tanker traffic offshore. And now there is a greater focus on oil-spill prevention." But he also said he wouldn't be shocked if a major spill occurred on his watch.

AND YET DESPITE these looming threats, sea otters are still chugging along, like the proverbial little engine that could. Whether they will continue on that road is a question to which the leading sea otter biologists have very different answers.

Jim Estes called the growing otter numbers in Southeast Alaska and British Columbia "a positive sign for the future." But he said so with a tone of dread in his voice because he fears for the animal's long-term survival, even where its populations seem healthiest today.

"There are more and more people, and more people means more human impact [on the environment], and more human impact is going to probably be bad for otters in one way or the other, especially in coastal zones where people tend to aggregate in higher densities," he said. "That's my worry. I think that as long as we have a global human population that is continuing to utilize more resources, we ought to worry about everything. Are otters high on that list of things to worry about? I think they're probably less high than a lot of species. . . . But the fact that sea otters live in such a very narrow habitat type—the coastal zone—and this coastal zone is a place where people tend to aggregate I think forewarns the potential for problems."

Estes's protégé, Tim Tinker, sees things a little differently. He admits he's more optimistic by nature than many other scientists, but his optimism stems from the sea otters' healthy recovery from the fur trade in much of their range. He said that even though humans did just about everything possible to wipe out sea otter populations two centuries ago, the animals have made a major comeback, despite a few hiccups along the way.

"Because of that big picture, I think they have a huge potential to recover," he said. "And more importantly, I think that they've taught us more about how ecosystems work and about the importance of predators in ecosystems than probably any other species. And that message is getting propagated now."

For many years, Tinker said, people thought predators were something that should be controlled or removed, but that belief is fast disappearing, thanks largely to what has been learned about the role of sea otters in their ecosystem.

"Although the nuances are different and they do different things in different areas, we haven't seen anywhere where they recover and nothing happens," he said. "Every time they recover, lots of big things happen, and in general it very often leads to increased biodiversity."

I hesitated before asking Tinker my last question. He had called himself "an unapologetic scientist" at a presentation he made at the annual meeting of the Friends of the Sea Otter, an indication that he can say only what the facts indicate. It's difficult for him to speculate, and it's even more difficult for him to make decisions that must factor in political considerations, economic realities, and public sentiments. So when I asked him what it would take to get sea otters to expand into Northern California and Oregon, to fill out their historic range, he started his answer with one simple fact. "We'd need to start another population."

And that's when he hedged, pointing out that starting another population of sea otters is not a decision for scientists like him to make. It's not even a question for wildlife managers or government regulators, he said. It's a question for society, especially for the people who live and work in those coastal communities.

"Do people in Humboldt County want to have sea otters in their marine ecosystem?" he asked. "They should be told very clearly that there would be impacts—if they have shellfisheries, there's going to be negative effects on shellfisheries. But on the other hand, they should be told that there would be increases in kelp and things that depend on kelp. They should get the whole story and make an informed decision.

"There is appropriate habitat all the way up the coast," he added. "I think that is a social question, a broad social question that should be made in an informed way, and that's the challenging part. There are those who want to sugarcoat it, and then there are those who want to make it sound as though it's like you're dropping a nuclear bomb, and neither of those extremes are true."

Regardless of whether the public has a chance to weigh in on that question, Tinker is confident that sea otters will continue to expand their range on their own.

"More importantly," he concluded, "I think they will continue to teach us about how ecosystems work a long way into the future. They've already taught us a ton, but they've only begun. There's so much more to learn from them."

Acknowledgments

MOST OF MY WRITING PROJECTS involve at least one field trip to join scientists at their research sites. Even when they take place in an office or laboratory, these adventures are always exciting. They're partly why I enjoy writing so much—it gives me an opportunity to go on the road to meet researchers and observe the scientific process as it happens. But a project like this book, a three-year undertaking involving more than a dozen field trips, requires the cooperation of a long list of scientists and other helpers. All of these individuals were generous with their time and happily (I think) shared their knowledge, expertise, and insights in a way that allowed me to turn them into what I hope is engaging prose for my audience of nonscientists. Any inaccuracies in the text are entirely my doing.

I am especially grateful to Tim Tinker, who somehow found time amid an immensely busy schedule of travel, research, writing, and teaching to spend many long hours with me in three different states over the course of two years. He patiently walked me through his complex research and provided me with some of my favorite wildlife adventures yet.

Numerous others—scientists, fishermen, and more—invited me into their homes, offices, and research sites; agreed to be interviewed; or shared vital information that found its way into this book. I am truly appreciative of their assistance. In Alaska, those people include Verena Gill, Marc Webber, Kristin Worman, George

Esslinger, Ginny Eckert, Zac Hoyt, Angela Doroff, Sunny Rice, Brett Long, Phil Doherty, Sonia Ibarra, Stephanie Jurries, Jim and Julie Alexander, Dave Beebe, Kathy Peavey, Dennis Nickerson, Mike Jackson, Peter Williams, Ben Weitzman, Matt Edwards, Brenda Konar, Craig Matkin, Doug Demaster, Dan Monson, Jim Bodkin, and Joel Garlich-Miller. In California, I am indebted to Lilian Carswell, Jim Curland, Laird Henkel, Melissa Miller, Andy Johnson, Karl Mayer, Angela Hains, Michelle Staedler, Sarah McKay Strobel, Zach Randell, Nicole Thometz, Lily Maxine Tarjan, Jim Estes, Tim Stephens, Brett Hughes, Sarah Espinosa, Gena Bentall, Brian Hatfield, Joe Tomoleoni, Mike Kenner, and Charles Kavanaugh.

I also owe thanks to Roger Dunlop, Martin Haulena, Lindsay Akhurst, Taryn Roberts, Sion Cahoon, Jonathan Hulquist, and Linda Nichol in British Columbia; Jessie Hale, Kristin Laidre, Steven Jeffries, Deanna Lynch, and Shawn Larson in Washington; Ron Jameson and Quinn Read in Oregon; and Katya Ovsyanikova in Russia. Thanks are also due to Beth Ullucci and the staff of the Jesse Smith Memorial Library, as well as to Peter August, Erica Tefft, Rodd Perry, Kim Robertson, Teresa Gervelis, and Cindy Sabato.

This is my fourth book about wildlife and natural history, and none of them would have gotten off the ground without the kindness and support of my literary agent, Charlotte Cecil Raymond, who has gracefully helped me navigate the publishing world and enthusiastically encouraged me throughout the research and writing process. Thanks also to my editor at Sasquatch Books, Gary Luke, and his fabulous staff.

And finally, I must once again recognize my wife, Renay, who offers whatever support I need whenever I need it, pulls me through bouts of worry and writer's block, never complains when I disappear on unplanned research trips, and leaves me alone when that appears to be the preferred strategy for success. I'm pleased— as she is—that she was able to join me for most of my sea otter adventures, earning her a prominent spot in several chapters of this book. All of my writing success is due to her encouragement, devotion, and understanding—not to mention her recent willingness to let me quit my job to write full time. I'm especially thankful to her for that.

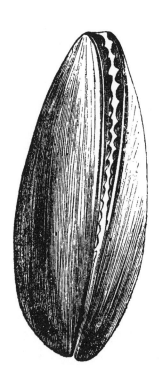

Selected Bibliography

Alonso, Mariana, M. L. Feo, C. Corcellas, L. G. Vidal, C. P. Bertozzi, J. Marigo, E. R. Secchi, et al. "Pyrethroids: A New Threat to Marine Mammals?" *Environment International* 47 (2012): 99–106.

Ames, J., J. Geibel, F. Wendell, and C. Pattison. "White Shark-Inflicted Wounds of Sea Otters in California, 1968–1992." *Great White Sharks* (1996): 309–16.

Ballachey, B. E., D. H. Monson, G. G. Esslinger, K. Kloecker, J. Bodkin, L. Bowen, and A. K. Miles. *2013 Update on Sea Otter Studies to Assess Recovery from the 1989 Exxon Valdez Oil Spill, Prince William Sound, Alaska.* Open-File Report 2014-1030. US Geological Survey.

Bockstoce, John R. *Furs and Frontiers in the Far North: The Contest Among Native and Foreign Nations for the Bering Strait Fur Trade.* New Haven: Yale University Press, 2009.

Bolin, Rolf. "Reappearance of the Southern Sea Otter along the California Coast." *Journal of Mammalogy* 19, no. 3 (1938): 301–303.

Bowen, Lizabeth, A. K. Miles, C. A. Holden, J. A. Saarinen, J. L. Bodkin, M. J. Murray, M. T. Tinker. "Effects of Wildfire on Sea Otter (*Enhydra lutris*) Gene Transcript Profiles." *Marine Mammal Science* 31 no. 1 (2015): 191–210.

Burek, K. A., V. A. Gill, and D. S. Bradway. "The First Case of Locally Acquired Disseminated Histoplasmosis in Alaska and in a Free-Ranging Marine Mammal." *Journal of Wildlife Diseases* 50 no. 2 (2014): 389–92.

Burris, O. E., and D. E. McKnight. *Game Transplants in Alaska: Wildlife Technical Bulletin No. 4.* Juneau: Alaska Department of Fish and Game, 1973.

California Legislature. *Effect of the Sea Otter on the Abalone Resource: Hearing Transcript of the California State Senate Fact Finding Committee, Subcommittee on Sea Otters.* San Luis Obispo. Nov. 19, 1963.

Clarke, Louise R., and Arthur H. Clarke. "Zooarchaeological Analysis of Mollusc Remains from Yuquot, British Columbia," edited by J. Dewhirst, in *The Yuquot Project* 2:37[1]57. Edited by W. J. Folan. Ottawa: Parks Canada, 1980.

Counihan-Edgar, Katrina, V. A. Gill, A. M. Doroff, K. A. Burek, W. A. Miller, P. L. Shewmaker, S. Jang, et al. "Genotypic Characterization of *Streptococcus infantarius* subspecies *coli* Isolates from Sea Otters with Infective Endocarditis and/or Septicemia and from Environmental Mussel Samples." *Journal of Clinical Microbiology* 50 no. 12 (2012): 4131–3.

Cox, Kenneth W. *California Abalones, Family Haliotidae: Fish Bulletin No. 118.* Resources Agency of California Department of Fish and Game, 1962.

DeGrange, Anthony R. *Conservation Plan for the Sea Otter in Alaska.* Anchorage: US Fish and Wildlife Service, 1994.

Demaster, Douglas P., Andrew W. Trites, Phillip Clapham, Sally Mizroch, Paul Wade, Robert J. Small, and Jay Ver Hoef. "The Sequential Megafaunal Collapse Hypothesis: Testing with Existing Data." *Progress in Oceanography* 68 no. 2-4 (2006): 329–42.

Doroff, Angela, Oriana Badajos, Karen Corbell, Dana Jenski, and Melanie Beaver. "Assessment of Sea Otter Diet in Kachemak Bay, Alaska." *IUCN Otter Specialist Group Bulletin* 29 no. 1 (2012): 15–22.

Doroff, Angela, and Oriana Badajos. *Monitoring Survival and Movement Patterns of Sea Otters in Kachemak Bay, Alaska.* Homer: Kachemak Bay Research Reserve, 2010.

Dubeya, J. P., and N. J. Thomas. "Sarcocystis neurona retinochoroiditis in a Sea Otter (*Enhydra lutris kenyoni*)." *Veterinary Parasitology* 183 (2011): 156–159.

Ebert, E. E. "A Food Habits Study of the Southern Sea Otter, *Enhydra lutris nereis*." California Department of Fish and Game 54 (1968): 33–42.

Eventon, Danielle. "Wildfires Cause Trouble for Sea Otters." KRCB. August 1, 2014.

Esslinger, G. G., and J. L. Bodkin. *Status and Trends of Sea Otter Populations in Southeast Alaska, 1969–2003*. US Geological Survey Scientific Investigations Report 2009–5045.

Estes, J. A. "Killer Whale Predation on Sea Otters Linking Oceanic and Nearshore Ecosystems." *Science* 282 no. 5388 (1998): 473–76.

Estes, J. A. *Serendipity: An Ecologist's Quest to Understand Nature.* Oakland: University of California Press, 2016.

Gibson, James R. *Otter Skins, Boston Ships, and China Goods: The Maritime Fur Trade of the Northwest Coast, 1785–1841*. Seattle: University of Washington Press, 1992.

Goldstein, T., J. A. K. Mazet, V. A. Gill, A. M. Doroff, K. A. Burek, and J. A. Hammond. "Phocine Distemper Virus in Northern Sea Otters in the Pacific Ocean, Alaska." *Journal of Emerging Diseases* 15 no. 6 (2009): 925–27.

Gordon, David G. *Field Guide to the Geoduck*. Seattle: Sasquatch Books, 1996.

Hughes, B. B., R. Eby, E. Van Dyke, M. T. Tinker, C. I. Marks, K. S. Johnson, and K. Wasson. "Recovery of a Top Predator Mediates Negative Eutrophic Effects on Seagrass." *Proceedings of the National Academy of Sciences* 110 no. 38 (2013): 15313–18.

Jameson, R. J., K. W. Kenyon, A. M. Johnson, and H. M. Wight. 1982. "History and Status of Translocated Sea Otter Populations in North America." *Wildlife Society Bulletin* 10: 100–107.

Jameson, R. J., K. W. Kenyon, Steven Jeffries, and Glenn R. VanBlaricom. "Status of a Translocated Sea Otter Population and Its Habitat in Washington." *The Murrelet* 67 no. 3 (1986): 84.

Jeffries, Steven, Deanna Lynch, and Sue Thomas. *Results of the 2015 Survey of the Reintroduced Sea Otter Population in Washington State*. Lakewood, WA: Washington Department of Fish and Wildlife, 2016.

Johnson, A., R. Jameson, T. Schmidt, and D. Calkins. *Sea Otter Survey, Southeast Alaska*. Anchorage: US Fish and Wildlife Service, 1983.

Jones, R. *Empire of Extinction: Russians and the North Pacific's Strange Beasts of the Sea, 1741–1867*. New York: Oxford University Press, 2014.

Kenyon, K. W. "The Sea Otter in the Eastern Pacific Ocean." *North American Fauna* 68 (1969).

Kvitek, R. G. and C. Bretz. "Harmful Algal Bloom Toxins Protect Bivalve Populations from Sea Otter Predation." *Marine Ecology Progress Series* 271 (2004): 233–43.

Laidre, Kristin L., Ronald J. Jameson, Eliezer Gurarie, Steven J. Jeffries, and Harriet Allen. "Spatial Habitat Use Patterns of Sea Otters in Coastal Washington." *Journal of Mammalogy* 90 no. 4 (2009): 906–17.

Lance, Monique M., Scott A. Richardson, and Harriet L. Allen. *Washington State Recovery Plan for the Sea Otter*. Olympia: Washington Department of Fish and Wildlife, 2004.

Larson, Shawn E., James L. Bodkin, and G. R. VanBlaricom. *Sea Otter Conservation*. London: Elsevier, 2015.

Larson, Sean D., Zachary N. Hoyt, Ginny I. Eckert, and Verena A. Gill. "Impacts of Sea Otter (*Enhydra Lutris*) Predation on Commercially Important Sea Cucumbers (*Parastichopus Californicus*) in Southeast Alaska." *Canadian Journal of Fisheries and Aquatic Sciences* 70 (2013): 1498–507.

Liwanag, Heather E. M., Annalisa Berta, Daniel P. Costa, Masako Abney, and Terrie M. Williams. "Morphological and Thermal Properties of Mammalian Insulation: The Evolution of Fur for Aquatic Living." *Biological Journal of the Linnean Society* 106 no. 4 (2012): 926–39.

Loomis, John B. *Economic Benefits of Expanding California's Southern Sea Otter Population*. Defenders of Wildlife, 2005.

Luk, Vivian. "Vancouver Aquarium Veterinarians Try to Save Sea Otter Suffering from Gunshot Wounds." *Vancouver Sun*. October 23, 2013.

Marshall, D. C., K. Rozas, B. Kot, and V. A. Gill. "Innervation Patterns of Sea Otter Mystacial Follicle-Sinus Complexes." *Frontiers of Neuroanatomy* 8 (2014): 121.

Maxwell, Gavin. *Ring of Bright Water*. New York: Dutton, 1961.

McGrath, Susan. "The Urchin Keepers." *Audubon*, January–February 2014, 38–45.

McNulty, Tim. "Washington's Otter Comeback." *Defenders Magazine*, Summer 1998.

Miller, Pam. *Nuclear Flashback: Report of a Greenpeace Scientific Expedition to Amchitka Island, Alaska—Site of the Largest Underground Nuclear Test in US History*. Greenpeace, 1996.

Mizroch, S. A., and D. W. Rice. "Have North Pacific Killer Whales Switched Prey Species in Response to Depletion of the Great Whale Populations?" *Marine Ecology Progress Series* 310 (2006): 235–46.

Owings, Margaret Wentworth. Oral history by Suzanne Riess and Ann Lage. "Artist, and Wildlife and Environmental Defender." Berkeley: Regional Oral History Office, Bancroft Library, University of California, 1991.

———. "Do Sea Otters Have Any Friends?" *Monterey Peninsula Herald*. March 11, 1968.

———. "The First Issue." *The Otter Raft* 1 (June 1969).

Palumbi, Stephen R., and Carolyn Sotka. *The Death and Life of Monterey Bay: A Story of Revival.* Washington, DC: Island Press, 2011.

Perlin, Ross. "Why Would Anyone Want to Shoot a Sea Otter?" *The Guardian.* March 10, 2015.

Pitcher, K. W. *Studies of Southeastern Alaska Sea Otter Populations: Distribution, Abundance, Structure, Range Expansion, and Potential Conflicts with Shellfisheries.* US Fish and Wildlife Service Cooperative Agreement No. 14-16-0009-954, Final Report Part I. Alaska Department of Fish and Game, 1989.

Recovery Plan for Southwest Alaska Distinct Population Segment of the Northern Sea Otter. Anchorage: US Fish and Wildlife Service, 2013.

Riedman, M. L., and J. A. Estes. "The Sea Otter (*Enhydra lutris*): Behavior, Ecology, and Natural history." *Biological Report* 90 no. 14 (1990).

Righthand, Jess. "Otters: The Picky Eaters of the Pacific." *Smithsonian.* September 2011.

Schneider, K. B., *Survey of Transplanted Sea Otter Populations in Southeast Alaska, April 30–May 16, 1975.* Anchorage: Alaska Department of Fish and Game, 1975.

Sea Otter Hides: What Is Significantly Altered? Anchorage: US Fish and Wildlife Service, 2014.

Sinnott, Richard. "Waiting for Mutiny on Proposed Southeast Alaska Sea Otter Bounty." *Alaska Dispatch News* (Anchorage, AK). March 25, 2013.

Southern Sea Otter Recovery Plan. Portland: US Fish and Wildlife Service Regional Office, 1982.

Springer, A. M., J. A. Estes, G. B. Van Vliet, T. M. Williams, D. F. Doak, E. M. Danner, K. A. Forney, and B. Pfister. "Sequential Megafaunal Collapse in the North Pacific Ocean: An Ongoing Legacy of Industrial Whaling?" *Proceedings of the National Academy of Sciences* 100 no. 21 (2003): 12223–28.

Steinbeck, John. *Cannery Row*. New York: Viking, 1945.

Thometz, Nicole M., M. T. Tinker, M. M. Staedler, K. A. Mayer, and T. M. Williams. "Energetic Demands of Immature Sea Otters from Birth to Weaning: Implications for Maternal Costs, Reproductive Behavior and Population-level Trends." *Journal of Experimental Biology* 217 (2014): 2053–61.

Tinker, M. T., B. B. Hatfield, M. D. Harris, and J. A. Ames. "Dramatic Increase in Sea Otter Mortality from White Sharks in California." *Marine Mammal Science* 32 (2015): 309–26.

Trites, Andrew W., Volker B. Deecke, Edward J. Gregr, John K. B. Ford, and Peter F. Olesiuk. "Killer Whales, Whaling, and Sequential Megafaunal Collapse in the North Pacific: A Comparative Analysis of the Dynamics of Marine Mammals in Alaska and British Columbia following Commercial Whaling." *Marine Mammal Science* 23 no. 4 (2007): 751–65.

"Slime-Producing Molecules Help Spread Disease from Cats to Sea Otters." University of California, Davis, News and Information. October 14, 2014. https://www.ucdavis.edu /news/slime-producing-molecules-help-spread-disease-cats-sea-otters.

"Sea Otters Promote Recovery of Seagrass Beds." University of California, Santa Cruz, Office of Public Affairs. August 26, 2013. http://news.ucsc.edu/2013/08/sea-otters-seagrass.html.

Wade, Paul R., Vladimir N. Burkanov, Marilyn E. Dahlheim, Nancy A. Friday, Lowell W. Fritz, Thomas R. Loughlin, Sally A. Mizroch, et al. "Killer Whales and Marine Mammal Trends in the North Pacific: A Re-Examination Of Evidence For Sequential Megafauna Collapse and the Prey-Switching Hypothesis." *Marine Mammal Science* 23 no. 4 (2007): 766–802.

Wild, P. W., and J. A. Ames. "A Report on the Sea Otter, *Enhydra lutris*, in California." *Marine Resources Technical Report*, no. 20, 1974.

Williams, Terrie M., and Randall William Davis. *Emergency Care and Rehabilitation of Oiled Sea Otters: A Guide for Oil Spills Involving Fur-Bearing Marine Mammals.* Fairbanks: University of Alaska Press, 1995.

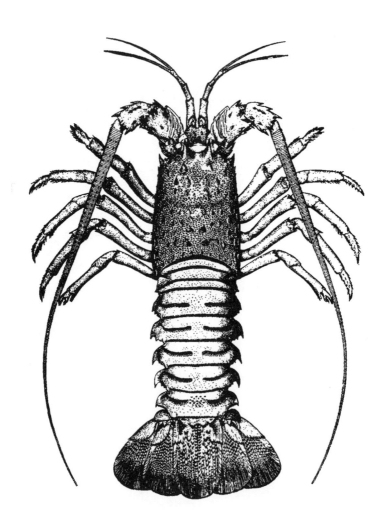

About the Author

TODD MCLEISH is a New England–based science writer who has written hundreds of newspaper, magazine, and website articles about wildlife and other environmental topics. His subjects have included dozens of endangered species, common backyard creatures, and issues such as offshore wind energy, invasive species, and marine debris. He is the author of three previous natural-history books: *Golden Wings & Hairy Toes*, *Basking with Humpbacks*, and *Narwhals: Arctic Whales in a Melting World*. Todd lives with his wife and two cats in Burrillville, Rhode Island.